Alexander Macleod

Our own lives

The Book of Judgment

Alexander Macleod

Our own lives
The Book of Judgment

ISBN/EAN: 9783743348912

Manufactured in Europe, USA, Canada, Australia, Japa

Cover: Foto ©Lupo / pixelio.de

Manufactured and distributed by brebook publishing software (www.brebook.com)

Alexander Macleod

Our own lives

OUR OWN LIVES

THE BOOKS OF JUDGMENT.

OUR OWN LIVES

THE BOOKS OF JUDGMENT.

BY

ALEXANDER MACLEOD, D.D.

> 'There the action lies
> In his true nature; and we ourselves compelled,
> Even to the teeth and forehead of our faults,
> To give in evidence.'

SECOND THOUSAND.

EDINBURGH:
ANDREW ELLIOT, 15, PRINCES STREET.
1869.

MURRAY AND GIBB, EDINBURGH,
PRINTERS TO HER MAJESTY'S STATIONERY OFFICE.

PREFACE.

IN the Moral Philosophy class of Glasgow University, about twenty-five years ago, our professor was in the habit of giving a short series of lectures annually, on the relation of Memory to the Moral Faculties. In the course of these lectures, he drew the attention of his students to Coleridge's suggestive hint, that 'memory might be the dread book which is to be opened at the day of judgment.' I have still a vivid recollection of the excitement, the joy of a new insight, which thrilled over the class that year I was a member of it, when the learned professor, looking kindly at the suggestion, went on to illustrate and confirm it by reflections and observations of his own.

What wonder if, among the earliest public efforts of the future preachers who then attended that class, the attempt to work out, for the purposes of religious instruction, the speculation which had given such delight to themselves, should have found a place! I can hardly doubt that many of my classmates besides myself tried their hand upon the tempting theme.

In my attempt, however, I did not find that Coleridge's hint carried me quite so far as I expected. It helped me, indeed, to develop memory as a record which might be used in the processes of the judgment; but somehow, when my lecture was finished, it was only the *dark* leaves of the record which had come out to view. It was not difficult to show how the guilt and sin in human life, the materials on which *condemnation* must rest, could be reproduced by memory. But the faith, the love, the goodness of the righteous,—how could the reproduction of these, *by this faculty*, constitute a judgment-book for them? Were good souls simply to remember that they had been good? It was against the whole spirit of the dispensation of grace, that the mere recollection of good deeds should be appealed to, as the evidence on which the awards to the righteous would be given. The speculation of the philosopher was good for a part, not for the whole: for the dark, not for the bright portion of the awful record. Moreover, it proceeded on the assumption that there is to be only *one* book of judgment; while the statements in Scripture, which it was intended to illustrate, make it plain that there are to be, at the very least, *two* such books. 'The books were opened, and *another book* was opened, which is the book of life.' On the first of these the philosopher seemed to shed a real light. The second he did not so much as touch. In the one, the active principle is, or may be, *memory*. In the other, it is certainly and only *life*.

After a few years the subject came back upon me, and I worked out, as a companion discourse to that which I had given 'upon the books,' the illustration of the second judicial record,—'the book of life.' To my surprise, and I may confess, vexation, I found myself a second time in the presence of an uncompleted theme. Here were the books of the final judgment, but where were the similar instruments of the ordinary judgments of providence? If there are, in the revealed word, book-symbols of the one, are there no similar symbols of the other? I need not lengthen out these details further, by explaining how I came to be satisfied that 'the book sealed with seven seals,' and 'the little book open,' mentioned in the earlier portions of the Apocalypse, were the symbols of which I felt the want, and the first half of a fourfold symbol, which covers the entire area of retribution.

The pages which follow contain a free rendering and illustration of the facts and principles of which those several 'books' are the symbols. They have been written under the conviction, that the symbols are organically related; that the judicial element characterizes each; that the 'sealed' and 'open' books symbolize facts *in the ordinary prelusive judgments of Providence,* and 'the books' and 'book of life' similar facts *in the great judgment at the end of the world.*

At the same time I am anxious to say, that, although worked out by the aid of symbols which occur in the Apocalypse, my little volume advances no claim to be received as 'Apocalyptic exposition.' The few pages, scattered here and there—not more than a dozen in all—which may seem to impart this character to my work, are merely the loopings-up of its several parts,—the links to indicate, or prove, the unity of my theme. My aim is the illustration of certain laws of retribution. The symbols by which I work have suggested the illustration. But these symbols are not confined to the Apocalypse. And there is nothing advanced, so far as I am aware, which might not have been drawn from other portions of Scripture.

My subject covers, I have had occasion to say, 'the entire area of retribution.' It would be very great presumption in any one to attempt an exhaustive treatment of a theme so ample. It underlies, and would exact, a complete history of the race. I offer only a few familiar illustrations,—a hint here and another there: the suggestion rather than the completion of the attempt.

It can be nothing new to thoughtful readers, that good and evil are subject to law; that their results are inscribed on the lives of those in whom they find a home; or that judgment over all the spheres they occupy is administered by Christ. The laws of retribution are old acquaintances of our race; and the deepest thoughts we are likely to have regarding them have probably been reached and expressed thousands of years ago. But this does not affect the duty of studying these laws. This cannot grow old. And we may gain a certain freshness of view and impression by looking at old facts through new mediums, especially if the mediums be as suggestive and true as 'the books of judgment.'

For the suggestion, and a portion of the proof, that the 'sealed book' is a book of judgment, I am indebted to Hengstenberg. What has been said by other writers, in elucidation of 'the books' (Part Fourth), I have already indicated in this Preface, and in the fullest way exhibited in the concluding chapters of the volume.

Christmas 1865.

Except the expansion of the Title, so as better to announce the character of the Contents, and the prefixing of an Analytical Table of Contents, to give a bird's-eye view of them, this volume remains every way as it was. I am under a great debt of obligation to those who have reviewed it, and return them here my cordial thanks for their favourable criticisms.

A. M'L.

BIRKENHEAD, *March* 1869.

CONTENTS.

Part First.

THE SEALED BOOK; OR, BOOK OF PRELUSIVE JUDGMENT.

I. THE SEER.

John in Patmos—His circumstances representative—The suffering Church—Mystery, depth, and extent of her sufferings—Her outlook into the future—Temptation to despair—In this situation, the Vision of the Sealed Book vouchsafed, . 3

II. THE SONG OF THE BOOK.

Retribution on the Church's foes the main feature in this Vision—Proof from the Song, which is the heart of the Vision, that the Sealed Book is specifically a Book of Judgment, and Christ the Administrator of the judgments inscribed in it, . 8

III. THE BOOK AND ITS INSCRIPTION.

The Book is *the life* of the evil-doer—Natural consequences of sin—The 'pen of iron.'—Sin writes its autographs on the being of the sinner—Illustrations: debasement of our noblest faculty by licentiousness; darkening of the moral sense of a community by slavery; suspension of the Church's usefulness by faction; deterioration of a race by idolatry; the lesson of a place of graves—Death by sin, ... 21

IV. THE SEALS.

The argument for the *future* judgment should not distract our minds from the *current* judgments of Providence—These judgments, *as such,* often sealed up from our view—Our limited knowledge is one seal—Our subjection to sense, another—Our mistaken conceptions regarding the time and nature of retribution, make a third and·fourth—Behind all these seals retribution on evil constantly at work—The Jewish nation and the heathen world, in the days of our Lord and the Apostles, illustrative of the fact—The Future a fifth seal—The Papal Church in this country on the eve of the Reformation.—Application of these facts to the present sufferings of the Church—The conflict of good and evil in our day—How long?—Our comfort in knowing that the Book is in the hands of Christ, ... 40

V. DISCLOSURES.

Prelusions—Cycles of judgment—Judgment days occurring continually—Disclosure of David's iniquity—Ananias and Sapphira—Evil cannot hide itself out of Christ's sight—Recent criminal trial—Judicial proof—A greater proof in the life of the murderer—The murder itself the fruit and natural outcome, the manifestation and therefore real disclosure of the man's sin—The evil-doer *becoming the evil* which he does, . . 61

Part Second.

THE OPEN BOOK; OR, BOOK OF THE JUDGING WORD.

I. THE LIGHT OF THE WORLD.

Characteristic circumstances of the Vision, in which the Open Book is displayed, lead to the conclusion that this second book is *the Book of the judging Word*—First, *Christ* Himself as the

Incarnate Word—Next, *His Gospel,* or spoken Word—Finally, *His Life,* as an embodied Word in the life of His people—This WORD brings with it a twofold issue: Accepted, it brings redemption; Rejected, judgment—The symbols in the Vision corroborative of this view, and illustrative of the fact, that it is *the history of Gospel preaching, in its effects on those who reject it,* we have to do with in the vision of the Open Book, . 79

II. THE LIGHT REVEALING THE DARKNESS.

Description of 'the World'—Its unconsciousness of the darkness it contains—The World's life in its sources—In its manifestations—Worldliness in social life—First effect of preaching in such a state of things—Revelation of the darkness, . . 91

III. THE DARKNESS HATING THE LIGHT.

Next effect of the Gospel on the World—Excites its hatred—The darkness is now revealed to itself—Hatred and persecution of the light begin to arise—Treatment our Lord received, an illustration of this—Deepening shadow of the hatred He evoked—His cruel death the natural result, . . . 98

IV. OUTER DARKNESS.

After the first outbreak of the World's hatred, the truth appears in the form of a *cause*—Those who live on the scene of the conflict are now compelled to take their places on the side of truth or error—To those who choose the side of error, everything contrives to thrust them deeper into its gloom, until at last they are utterly *outside* of the sphere of light—It is with the rejection of the Gospel as with the doomed captives at a Roman triumph: the very Gospel to them is a 'savour of death unto death,' 104

Part Third.

DISCIPLINE; OR, REVELATIONS OF WRATH ON THE WAY OF LIFE.

I. IN THE DEEPS.

The place of wrath in the processes of redemption, a fire of cleansing as well as of wrath—Discipline—Spiritual history of a generation—A revival—Awakening of anxiety—Souls in the presence of the Judge—Conviction of sin, . . . 113

II. BENEATH THE CROSS.

What convinced sinners behold in the cross is a Saviour wounded for their transgressions—Christ 'crucified' a revelation of judgment as much as mercy—He is a Judgment Book, inscribed with sinners' doom—Conversion, ... 119

III. PERFECTING HOLINESS.

Chastisement—Christ's wrath on the sins of His flock—Laying bare the handwriting of sin in the life—*Our* God a consuming fire, ... 122

IV. CONTENDING WITH WRONG.

The Christian conflict with wrong-doing—Christian exposure and reprobation of evil, a revelation of the Divine anger—Corn-law struggle—Condition of the poor in great cities—The Divine purpose in pestilence, ... 126

V. THE END.

Visible retributions on wrong-doing—In India—In Italy—A generation, at the end of its spiritual history and probation, before the Judge—Separation of the righteous and the wicked—Appearance of the wicked, 'filled with their own devices'—The wicked have *become* a book of judgment, . . 132

Part Fourth.

THE BOOKS; OR, THE MEMORIES OF THE JUDGED.

I. ANALOGY AND SCRIPTURE.

Records of our lives kept by God—The judged must know the grounds on which the judgment proceeds—All the appliances of the judicial process in man's own being—The recording faculty, or memory—Scripture proofs, ... 141

II. THE RECORDING ANGEL.

Fitness of memory for the purposes of a judgment book—Recording, preserving, and reproducing powers of memory—The old man recalling the scenes of his youth—Associative power of ideas—Operations of this power in reproducing the contents of memory—Can that power be so wielded that the entire past of our lives can be disclosed at once? 149

III. THE FACE OF THE JUDGE.

The place and power of conscience in our moral history—It is a witness of all we do—It is also our inner representative of God—Up to our knowledge of God, the conscience is the Face of God turned on our life—Revelation and power of the Face of Christ on the judgment day—Conscience the Face of God to the eye of faith—Christ at His coming to judge the world, the Face of God to the eye of sense—The vision of the Judge's person on the throne, and the Judge's word in the conscience, one—At the appearance of Christ, in consequence, every action of our lives shall be recollected, ... 158

IV. OPENING OF THE BOOKS.

The resurrection body—Enlargement and elevation of mental faculties—Operations of memory in the new circumstances—The pages of the past opened in the recollections of the ungodly—The pleasant reminiscences of the righteous, . . . 166

Part Fifth.

THE BOOK OF LIFE; OR, BOOK OF THE MANIFESTATION OF THE SONS.

I. A FAMILY REGISTER.

Difference between 'Book of Life' and 'The Books'—It is pre-eminently *the* book of the righteous—It is the book written in heaven—It is a family register—The names inscribed in it those of God's people only, ... 177

II. THE NAMES ON THE BOOK.

The *names* a part of the symbol—They represent *spiritual character*—Illustrations from Scripture names—Baptism into the name of God—In what sense 'The Lamb's book'—Name and life—In what sense a 'book of life'—Christ *the* life and name of God—Christ the formative principle of all true life—Christian life, in consequence, a book of *life*, ... 183

III. FORMATION OF CHARACTER.

Action of the life on the body—Illustration from the effects of evil—Corresponding effects on the side of good—Spirit pressing into form, and into bodily form—The face, walk, bearing of a Christian—Truth in the heart reveals itself as beauty in the body—Mrs. Fry in the Newgate cell—The transfiguration of our Lord an illustration of this law—The transforming power of the Holy Ghost in the life, ... 191

IV. MANIFESTATIONS.

The resurrection is the judicial opening of the books—The wicked raised in the bodies they defiled and debased, all scarred and spotted with sin—The righteous in the beautiful bodies which the Holy Spirit has been forming since the day of their conversion—The 'manifestation' of the sons: their glorious appearance, ... 199

V. THE BIBLE OF THE WORLD TO COME.

The people of Christ one, as their life is one—Their several names, or characters, only syllables of the One threefold name of God—Looked at in their wholeness, they are the manifestation of God's name and mighty work in redeeming them—The 'elect number'—The 'perfect man,' different names for this unity—The completion of it a *new revelation of God*—Probable purposes of that revelation in the future—The Bible of the world to come, ... 204

VI. POSTSCRIPT.

Self and Christ—Better to have our names written in the Book of Life than to have success in any work—The wisdom of accepting the place God gives us—The glory of the humblest place among the names of the Book of Life, ... 214

Part Sixth.

MEMORY AND CONSCIENCE.

AN APPENDIX

Chiefly illustrative of the Fourth and Fifth Parts.

I. THE CONTENTS OF MEMORY: Views of Augustine, . 221

II. THE IMPERISHABLENESS OF MEMORY: Views of Coleridge and De Quincey, ... 227

III. REMEMBERING IN THE FUTURE: Views of Jeremy and Isaac Taylor, ... 236

IV. CONSCIENCE: Dr. Whewell's description, . . . 245

V. EXTERNAL TESTIMONY: Speculations of Babbage and Hitchcock, ... 249

Part First.

THE SEALED BOOK,

OR,

THE BOOK OF PRELUSIVE JUDGMENT.

' I saw in the right hand of Him that sat on the throne a book written within and on the back side, sealed with seven seals.'

John.

'Then I turned, and lifted up mine eyes, and looked, and behold a flying roll. And he said unto me, What seest thou? And I answered, I see a flying roll; the length thereof is twenty cubits, and the breadth thereof ten cubits. Then said he unto me, This is the curse that goeth forth over the face of the whole earth.'

Zechariah.

' The sin of Judah is written with a pen of iron, and with the point of a diamond: it is graven upon the table of their heart, and upon the horns of your altars.'
' They that depart from me shall be written in the earth.'

Jeremiah.

' If any man worship the beast and his image, and receive his mark in his forehead, or in his hand, the same shall drink of the wine of the wrath of God, which is poured out without mixture into the cup of his indignation.'

Reb. XIV.

I.

THE SEER.

'When first written, the book of Revelation was destined to suit the peculiar circumstances of the early Christians. Persecution had appeared in various forms. The followers of Christ were exposed to severe suffering for conscience sake. Their enemies were fierce against them. Comparatively few and feeble, the humble followers of the Lamb seemed doomed to destruction.'

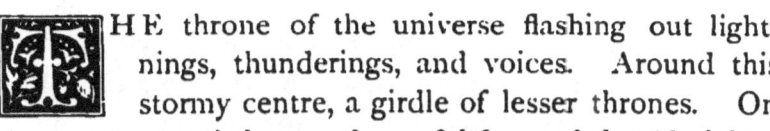HE throne of the universe flashing out lightnings, thunderings, and voices. Around this stormy centre, a girdle of lesser thrones. On the great central throne, the awful form of the Almighty, with a sealed Book in His right hand. On the inferior thrones, twice twelve crowned and white-robed men—the representatives of the redeemed. And, in front of all, an angel, crying with a loud voice, 'Who is worthy to open the Book, and to loose the seals thereof?'

Revelation puts on her splendid apparel only when the need of God's people is great. In desolate Patmos John's need was very great. Banishment, slavery, and chains—a convict's place in the imperial mines—expressed the world's estimate of the Master to whose service he had consecrated his life.

In the evolutions of providence, during times of persecution, there is ever a solemn moment for the persecuted

—the moment which precedes the manifestation, to their consciousness, of the power and presence of their Lord. This is the moment which is represented in this vision, at the point where its action concentrates on the sealed Book. The eyes of the Seer behold the mystery; but not yet the light in which it is to be dissolved. His gaze is turned towards the great throne at the centre. His soul is brooding on one question, which must find its solution there. That mysterious Roll lying on the right hand of Him who sits upon the throne; that Book sealed with seven seals, and written within and on the back side? Is the mystery which its seals enclose to be laid bare? Are the things written within its folds to be made known? The lorn exile wept because no man was found worthy to open and read the Book. He knew the tremendous issues involved. He knew that the vision was dealing with the fortunes of the cause for which he suffered. The challenge of the angel, 'Who is worthy to open the Book?' was simply the questioning of his own soul, taken apart from himself, translated into the language of symbol, and transfigured to his view in heaven. He, too, in his sorrow had flung forth this very appeal. He had carried the burden it expressed for years. Under the pressure of persecution, when his own way, and the way of the Church, was hedged up with suffering, he had sent up his cry for light. Was 'the man of the earth' to go on trampling the cause of Christ? Were the wicked to be lords for ever? Was the truth to be trodden, as it had been, under the hoof of the world? Was no hour of retribution, no arm of deliverance, to arise? In his old age, in dreary Patmos, was he to rest in the sorrowful thought that the glorious dawn for the earth and man, which his youth had witnessed, was never to kindle into a perfect day? 'I wept much because no man was found worthy to open and read the book, neither to look thereon.'

The tears of the apostle, like everything else in his circumstances, were representative. He wept, as God's people in all ages have had to do, in the presence of the great mysteries of providence. The old psalmists, staggering in their faith at the sight of the prosperity of the wicked, and John weeping in Patmos, reveal the same situation. In either case, a righteous soul is driven into strait places by the persecution of men, or driven so hard as to put the sorrowful, almost despairing, question, 'If the foundation be destroyed, what can the righteous do?'

With the flock it fared as with the shepherd, and even worse. John heard only the first mutterings of the storm. The Church of the Apostles was cradled in a persecution which seemed to grow more violent as the years went on. Its path from the beginning was one of trial and suffering. The times were adverse. The powers which ruled the world were jealous. And in relation to the claims of the Church, even the claims for bare place and freedom, the whole earth was an inhospitable waste.

We require, indeed, to put forth a continuous effort of thought, to appreciate and thoroughly realize the relations, in which the early Christians stood to the world of their time. They were a poor, broken, and scattered flock in a land of wolves. Their teachers were counted worthy of bonds and jails, of scourging and death. Teachers and followers, they seemed pledged to a hopeless cause.

Persecution lay heavy on their life. The present was dreary; the outlook into the future must have seemed drearier still. What were they, to carry the burden of such an outlook? And how terrible were their foes! It was a contrast between the feeblest and mightiest things which could be named. On the one side, little bands of believing souls; on the other, the whole Roman empire. On the one side, poverty, inexperience, humble circumstances; on the other, the wealth, the craft, and the power of a world. On the one side, holiness and suffering; on the other, hoary superstition, pride, cruelty, and brute force. What a sea for the fragile bark! Waves of blood, of persecution, of scorn—the whole wrath of the whole wicked world—rolling in with threatening crests on their very path!

We think of Rome and Roman persecution as things of the past. To the early Christians they were the harsh realities of the present. To us they are mere history; to them they were actual scourging, actual imprisonment, actual crucifixion. As far as this life was concerned, their prospect must have been one of tremendous and deep-seated gloom. The future must have seemed to stretch out in sad continuation of the very horrors they were enduring. East, west, north, and south—wherever the heralds of the gospel might penetrate—they saw nothing but a Roman world. What could to-morrow be, unless the Lord should suddenly return, but a continuation of to-day? No sign as yet told the simple followers of the Lamb, that from the very bark which carried them a Voice should go forth to all the surging and towering wrath which threatened them, with an all-powerful

'Peace, be still!' No Tacitus had appeared to *them* to point out, over all the dominions of the vast empire which persecuted them, the elements of approaching ruin. No prophet arose to tell them, that wastes and woods, unknown to the geography of the times, were rife with the mustering hordes of Goth and Vandal. Imperial armies seemed to fill the future with their perpetual tread. Imperial jails lifted their gloomy walls amid all the cities of the Time-to-come. The grim cross flung out its arms on every eminence, along all the highways of the human race. And cruel and pagan Rome, to human eyes, was still to be lord of all.

This was the situation—present, or near at hand—of the apostle and the Church, when Christ revealed for their consolation, the spectacle in which the Sealed Book is displayed.

II.

THE SONG OF THE BOOK.

'Thou art worthy to take the book, and to open the seals thereof: for Thou wast slain, and hast redeemed us to God by Thy blood out of every kindred, and tongue, and people, and nation: and hast made us unto our God kings and priests: and we shall reign on the earth.'

INTO all the manifold significance, teaching, and high forecastings of providence, which are disclosed, or meant to be disclosed, in this sublime vision, I have neither the qualifications necessary, nor the wish, to enter here. My limited purpose restricts me to the mystery of the book, which lay on the right hand of God. Of this, and only of this,—of its function, its inscriptions, and seals,—I intend to speak. I wish to show what the book represents; and how, if for us as for John it is still a sealed book, it is also, no less entirely, subject to the control of Christ, to inscribe, to keep shut, or to unseal, as the critical moments of His providence may demand. A brief statement or two will be sufficient to loosen the symbolic wrapping, and disclose the reality it represents, in its practical and every-day aspect.

I notice first, that under any really feasible interpretation, the judicial element must, directly or indirectly, be included. Different minds have discerned in this symbol 'the Book of the Secret Decrees of God;' 'the Book of Destiny;' 'the Book of the Inheritance;' 'the Book of Universal History;' 'the Book of the Future;' or 'the Book of Providence.' But every one of these interpretations—different but not contradictory—carries a reference to judgment in its right hand. Whatever else it may be, it certainly is a book of judgment. Whatever more may be 'written within and on the back side,' the handwriting of Christ against His enemies is undoubtedly there. Its very position, it has been well shown, is an indication of its judicial character. It lies 'in the right hand of Him who sat upon the throne;' in that hand 'which teaches terrible things,' and is 'full of righteousness,' and at which Christ is set 'until His enemies are made His footstool.' It is such a book also, that the opening of its seals is the revelation, or issuing, of judgments upon the earth. As each seal is opened, ministers of divine retribution are seen going forth. Mysterious riders, on symbol-coloured horses, ride in among the nations with commissions of wrath. One of the riders is Death. His aide-de-camp is Hell. As they ride, destruction falls down along their path. Conquest, and civil war, and famine, and wild beasts, are let loose. In the very heart of the vision, and after the unloosing of one of the seals, rises the cry of the persecuted people of God—'the souls of them that were slain for the word of God.' It is a cry for judgment, for swifter judgment. 'How long, O Lord, how long?' The wheels of the Judge's chariot are too long of coming. In answer to this cry, earthquakes, and black suns, and moons of blood, and falling stars, and trembling and despair among men, pass forward upon the scene. Effects like these could only follow the opening of a Book of Judgment.

I observe next, that everything in the vision, in which this symbol occurs, seems to speak to us of the domain of providence. Those prelusions of the consummation of all things, of which providence is so full, salute us here. The circumstances prefigure those of the judgment-day. The throne is an earnest of the great white throne; the sealed book of the books, which are on that day to be opened; and Christ's possession of the book is the embodiment of the fact, that, as in the end, so in these prelusions of the end, 'judgment has been committed to the Son.' As possessor of the book, He occupies the throne, and is the object of the homage of all creation, and of angels as well as men. So far as the attributes of His person are symbolized, they point to Him who in providence makes all things 'work together for good' to those who love Him. It is the 'Lamb,' the redemptive heart of providence; the 'Lion,' the avenging arm of providence; the 'root of David,' the kingly power in providence,—who prevails to open the book. He is the Lord mighty to save or destroy, for the redeemed in glory ascribe their redemption to Him, and the oppressed on earth appeal to Him for the avenging of their wrongs. And finally, His power to deal with this great mystery of time, the oppression of the righteous by the wicked, is represented as a joy to all who are embraced in the great scheme of providence. All this seems to confirm, not only the general conclusion, that the sealed book is a book of judgment, but also, to carry us on to this further specific fact, that it is, as distinguished from the books of the final judgment, the book of the ordinary prelusive judgments of Providence.

But, that I may not assume what ought to be proved, or seem to put a mere fancy of my own into the field from which I should rather seek to dig up the thoughts of God, I shall turn, for a moment or two, to a proof of the judicial character of the book, which may possibly carry the more conviction with it, that it is indirect. The song which is addressed to the Lord of the book is precisely such a song as His possession of judicial power might be expected to evoke from His worshippers. The soul of the Apocalypse comes out in its acts of worship. If we can catch the tone or reach the underlying element of any of those acts; if, looking with the eyes of the worshippers, we can place before our minds that special aspect of the Redeemer which has kindled them into song, we shall have the real secret of that particular vision in our grasp. This is the test which I am anxious to apply at present. If the book sealed with seven seals be, as I allege, a judgment book, the worship addressed to Him, who had power to open it, will have the throb of retribution at its heart.

It should be borne in mind that this worship, like the vision in which it occurs, was revealed as consolation for John. He was in tears because no man could unseal the book.

It is a most suggestive fact, that the first word of the consolation comes from one of the representatives of the redeemed. It was one of the elders who said to the exile, 'Weep not!' To that elder and his companions the seals on the book had caused no anxiety. The secret of the Lord was in their hearts. They knew, that there was One eye from which the things written in that book were never hid; One mind for which the shadow which had perplexed the soul of the apostle had no terror. 'The Lion of the tribe of Juda, the Root of David, *He* hath prevailed to open the book.' At the mention of this fact, and from this moment forward, the whole aspect of the vision changes. As on a day of excessive brightness, the objects in the distance come slowly and one by one within the scope of the dazzled eye, so this scene of heavenly vision seems to expand as the eyes of the Seer become used to its light. New splendours, unnoticed before, start into view. Like the young man in Elisha's day, his eyes are opened, and he sees heaven filled with the hosts and creatures of God, and better than all, with the presence of the Lamb.

In the light which breaks upon him now, the tears of the captive-prophet have disappeared. The mystery which lay upon his soul is unloosed. The book is in the hands of his Lord.

'What no man in heaven, nor in earth, nor under the earth' could do, has been done by Christ. HE has prevailed 'to open the book, and to loose the seven seals.' The joy of the Seer seems to palpitate up into the throngs of heaven. The songs of the world which is interested when even one sinner repenteth on earth, leap forth to express his joy. Christ has prevailed to open the book ! All heaven and its inhabitants rejoice. The sky, which had been filled with tempest, is now resonant with song. The circles which had come so suddenly into view, are stirred and vocal with praise. From centre to circumference, the scene resounds with the voice of worship. In utterances, varying with the varying relations to redemption of those who take part in it, the praise swells outward, until it reverberates in the uttermost horizons of life. Men and angels, and all lower things, have their part in it. Those nearest the throne, the white-robed representatives of the Church, begin; the encompassing angels catch up the song, and roll it onwards in a chorus of their own. Its last utterances are sent back to the centre from the remotest depths and heights of created life.

In all this outburst of praise and exultation, the song of the twenty-four elders is evidently the song of the occasion. The songs of the angels and the creatures are but the complement of theirs. This is pre-eminently the Song of the Sealed Book. And if we would know the character of that book, we must open our minds to the thoughts which find expression in this song.

The song is first of all a song of thanks: 'Thou hast redeemed us.' The singers have come hither 'out of every kingdom, and tongue, and people, and nation.' Their song drains the thanks of a broad domain. From far-sundered countries, from nations unable to understand each other's speech, from races of every hue, they have been gathered by the Lamb. The power, which has accomplished so much, has impressed their hearts. Over all that area, had reached the arm which redeemed them. Amid the great throngs to which they belonged, Christ had searched them out. He had spoken to them in their native tongues. He had adapted himself to every peculiarity in their circumstances. He had wrestled with their spirits, and overcome them, and made them His own. There was such power in His sympathy, that it penetrated, and used for redemption purposes, every peculiarity of nature, and race, and sphere. There was such power in His grace, that it broke down, in their hearts, the might of indifference, and enmity, and lust, and sin. He had the might to translate them from the darkness and bondage of the evil condition, in which He found them at first, into the light, and liberty, and blessedness of their present state. There was no speech nor language where this Redeemer had not been heard: 'His line had gone out through all the earth, and His words to the end of the world.'

But the redemption they celebrate was specially a redemption from the oppression and cruelty of men. The elders, who sing this song, represent the multitude which has come up out of great tribulations. The hate and the malice of men had risen up to destroy them, and out of all their troubles this Lord had saved them. He had delivered them from the furnace, and the jaw of the lion, and had brought them into His own presence with joy upon their heads. In all this, there was judgment as well as redemption. There was a deliverance which implied conflict with evil, and victory over evil-doers, and punishment of evil deeds. It implied the baffling of the plans of the persecutor, and the confounding of his devices. It involved acts, which enter essentially into the functions of an avenger. By mighty acts, and with an outstretched arm, the Lord had redeemed His people. But the acts of that arm were acts of judgment on their foes. Their oppressors had been humbled, their persecutors thwarted, their false accusers put to shame. The arm of 'the man of the earth' had been smitten in its pride; and blindness, or madness, or feebleness, or death had descended on all the enemies of those who sing. Thus, from the background of their thankful joy, steps forward a witness for retribution.

Again, the song of the elders is more than personal thanksgiving. It is a prophecy of consolation as well. It is sung for John and the suffering Church. If it looks back to the oppressions, from which the worshippers themselves have been redeemed, it still more emphatically looks forward to 'what is behind of the afflictions,' which their brethren on earth have still to fill up. Read in this light, the song is the letting down of a heavenly harmony into the discords of the lot of the exile, who was permitted to hear it sung. It is the embodiment of the crowned and white-robed future which awaited his fellow-sufferers and himself. These singers had once, as really as John, sent up their bitter cry from under the altar, 'How long, O Lord, how long?' But their jubilant utterance now is, 'Thou hast redeemed us!' As these redeemed elders sing, the prisoner of Patmos shall one day also sing. The song is the utterance of souls who see that the kingdom, over which Christ rules, is one in which the positions of earth are reversed. The first are last and the last are first, in this new world to which they have been brought. 'Thou hast made *us* kings and priests.' On earth they had been neither kings nor priests. They were a poor, scattered, persecuted flock—just like John and his companions—driven by the cruel rage of man from city to city, dragged, as criminals and disturbers of the peace, before kings and priestly councils, and condemned for loving and serving Christ. But now it has all changed. Death, according to the awful prophecy in the forty-ninth Psalm, was 'feeding' upon their enemies. The strength of those who oppressed was consumed in the grave. And in this morning light of heaven, in this Christ-made world, where the wronged on earth are righted, the persecuted have the dominion. And 'we,'—Thy torn and trodden followers,—even '*we* shall reign on the earth.' And thus once more, under this second aspect of the song, we detect the beat of the great thought of a righteous retribution.

But it is in the third and highest element of the song, we come most closely into contact with this thought. Besides being personal thanksgiving and prophecy, the song of the redeemed is Worship of the Redeemer. And it is the judicial aspect of His work, they praise. The Object of this worship is seated on the throne of the universe. He is about to step forth on a great task of redemption and judgment. Those who worship Him in these circumstances, have seen deeds similar to those He is about to accomplish. They are a chorus foretelling the future by the past. 'Thou hast redeemed us.' The whole history of His government is disclosed in these words.

The song is often quoted as if it were an acknowledgment of His worth as a sacrifice: 'Thou art worthy . . . for Thou wast slain.' But it is more, by being less, than this. 'Thou art worthy *to take the book, and to open the seals thereof,* for Thou wast slain.' The fact that He was slain is celebrated here, only because it imparts the right to open the book. The singers take their stand on the fact that He is judge, because He is first of all sacrifice. He is worthy to unloose the seals of judgment, because He is the Lamb slain from the foundation of the world. We are accustomed to connect the death of Christ with the outflowings of His mercy: the connection here, is between that death and the outflowings of His justice. He died, therefore by Him we live. But no less—He died, therefore by Him we shall be judged. It is the two sides of the one prerogative. The right to receive the penitent and to condemn the impenitent is the same. Grace and judgment flow down from the cross. The cross is the basis of everything in the glory of Christ. His position as Mediator, His personal glory, His authority to execute judgment, His ultimate victory over all who oppose Him, find their root and explanation in His death. He is exalted, because He humbled Himself to the cross. 'He sat down at the right hand of the Majesty on high,' because 'He had by himself purged our sins.' This is the truth which gives its peculiar shape to this song. Because He was slain, He can do what no man in heaven, or on earth, could have done. He receives the book of judgment out of the right hand of the Father. By His death, He prevails to open that book. By that death, He gave to the broken law all it could claim; and by that law, He is now crowned Administrator of its decrees. From Calvary to the throne of judgment, the passage is one of right. And the right is in His blood. 'Thou art worthy to take the book, and to open the seals thereof; for Thou wast slain, and hast redeemed us to God by Thy blood.'

But all this vindicates, and illustrates, the judicial character of the book, which He alone was found worthy to open. The thoughts of this song are thoughts which belong to the domain of retribution, and such thoughts as might appropriately find place in worship addressed to the Judge of men. In the depths of this song, therefore, I find the great faith, that there is a Judge in the earth who judgeth righteously, and Christ the crucified is He. It is the grand reply of all the life He has redeemed, and of all the life He sustains, to the questionings and the darkness, to the perplexities and the longings of the world below. It is the joy of the old psalmists of earth, reproduced by the psalmists of heaven. Out of the heart of divine worship on earth, long ages before, had risen in dark days, the appeal to the heaven and the earth, and to hills and fields and floods, to rejoice in the blessed fact, that the Lord was Judge. And now, from the heart of divine worship in heaven, in yet darker days, the skies, and seas, and fields, and woods, and the everlasting hills, and angels, and redeemed men, make answer to the appeal, and rejoice in the presence and power of that Judge.

I have only further to add, in confirmation of this rendering of the Song of the Book, and of the view of Christ and the Book, to which it points, that the worship in this vision, belongs to a series of acts of worship, which are indubitably characterized by the elements of retribution. Although Christ is represented throughout as a 'Lamb,' it is as the Lamb from whose 'wrath' the wicked are to flee. The worshippers are either appealing to Him for vengeance on the foes of His Church, or thanking Him for judgments on evil-doers. The worship addressed to

Him is, for the most part, worship of the Judge and Avenger of the Elect. The ground thoughts of apocalyptic worship are the justice and authority of Christ, His right to administer judgment, and His power to deliver His people from their foes. You will search in vain for any traces of that sickly feeling, that Christ's exercise of the retributive function is inconsistent with His exercise of mercy. From the first announcement of the great subject of the Apocalypse, as 'He who cometh with clouds,' whom every eye is to see, until He is set forth before us, seated on the great white throne, through all the variety of worship He receives, He is represented as the Dispenser of retributions. The worshippers never put His justice into the background. It is as essential to their conception of His character as His mercy. His mercy and His justice, for them, are tides of the same sea of life. If these worshippers were ever troubled with the questions,—Whether He who supplicates mercy for His enemies, when they are mocking Him on the cross, can be the same who is to say, 'Depart from me, ye cursed, into everlasting fire?'—whether the hand which plunges into the fire, to snatch a brand from the burning, and the hand which kindles that fire, be one?—whether it be the same life, the same tone of life, which floods the heart of man with waves of tenderness, and smites the sinner in his sin?—they are troubled by such perplexities no longer. They are in an atmosphere where the shadows, which separate human insight into fragments, have no place. They draw their knowledge from the sources, where prophets and apostles drew their representations of 'the wrath of the Lamb.' Judgment and mercy lie together in their thoughts, as, in the Bible, the threatenings of the lake of fire, beside the mother-hearted calls of the gospel. They worship as those who know, that justice and mercy are the immutable points between which the pendulum of Divine righteousness oscillates, and that they are everlasting, in their conjunction and co-operation, in all the works of God.

And now, O Lamb of God, fountain of all mercy to them who receive Thee, treasury of all wrath to them who reject Thee, bestow upon us the most gracious influences of Thy Spirit, when we now, with humble and awe-filled hearts, and seeking only to know and represent Thy righteous acts, go forward to the study of that book whose seals Thou, and Thou only, hast prevailed to loose.

III.

THE BOOK AND ITS INSCRIPTIONS.

'No longer among individuals of the race is there equality or likeness, a distributed fairness and fixed type visible in each, but evil diversity and terrible stamp of various degradation; features seamed with sickness, dimmed by sensuality, convulsed by passion, pinched by poverty, shadowed by sorrow, branded with remorse; bodies consumed with sloth, broken down by labour, tortured by disease, dishonoured in foul uses; intellects without power, hearts without hope, minds earthly and devilish; our bones full of the sins of our youth; the heaven revealing our iniquity, the earth rising up against us; the roots dried up beneath, and the branch cut off above. Well for us only, if, after beholding this our natural face in a glass, we desire not straightway to forget what manner of men we be.'—

RUSKIN.

IT is a judgment book. But this is only to know its function. Of what other facts is this book the symbol? The symbolic element penetrates to the contents, and to the very substance, of the book. It is a book, a book-roll, a parchment. What does this parchment represent? What is that reality, the unloosing of whose seals is the revelation of retributions upon men? What is that sealed record, which is so entirely under the control of the Lamb, which receives and contains, until He reveals it, the handwriting of His wrath? What, stripped of its symbolic covering, is that awful document, whose place is the right hand of the Judge, and which is written all over with the dooms of evil-doers, written on both sides,—written like Ezekiel's roll within and without, and crowded 'with lamentations, and mourning, and woe?'

There are two directions in which we may turn for a reply to these questions. If we seek it in the Bible, we are met by a wonderfully varied and ample testimony to the fact, that the consequences of sin descend on the sinner himself. If we seek it among our own observations of what is taking place around us, we will find many and sad opportunities of confirming the testimony of Scripture. In either direction, we learn that we live in a world whose Maker has ordained, that evil-doers shall eat the fruit of their own ways, and be filled with their own devices. The same being who is the occasion, is also the subject of retribution. And thus, using the language of the symbol, we arrive at the fact, that the being of the sinner himself is the book, on which the Lord inscribes the wrath against his sin.

The circumstances under which many of the Psalms were written resembled those in which John received the vision of the sealed book. I have had occasion to refer to the eleventh Psalm, and recur to it now to point out the character of the consolation vouchsafed to its author. With a much more explicit and direct outshaping of facts, it is almost an anticipation of that displayed to John. Above the unrighteousness and inhumanity of earth, the Psalmist is made to see 'the Lord's throne in heaven,' and the great fact of providence, that 'His eyes behold and His eyelids try the children of men.' And then, he is assured that the wicked shall not go unpunished; that 'upon the wicked He shall rain fire, and brimstone, and an horrible tempest;' that this shall be the 'portion in their cup.' Let the things written in the sealed book, and the ingredients of this cup, be read as equivalents of each other. Translate the symbolism of the vision by the more familiar symbolism of the Psalm, and we are again in presence of the fact,—which is the true answer to the inquiries with which I set out,—that the life which is to drink the cup, and the parchment on which the hidden sentences are written, are one and the same reality; and that, in short, the underlying substance, symbolized in the parchment of the book, is *the life of the evil-doer.* 'The sin of Judah . . . is graven upon *the table of their heart.*' 'He that sinneth against me *wrongeth his own soul.*' This is that mysterious roll on which the gaze of heaven was fixed, which is sealed to every eye but Christ's. This is the page which receives the inscriptions of His wrath; the quick and sensitive medium, closed in time, or only partially opened, which at the last shall display His judgments upon evil-doers. Very literally a book, for it fulfils the purposes which a book fulfils; it receives and then reveals the handwriting of its author. But the reality represented by this book— the page or parchment which actually receives that handwriting—is nothing other, nothing lower, than *the life on which the retributions descend.*

I touch here the fact, of which all that follows is an illustration. The book I am to interpret is a living book. The judgments I am to decipher are judgments inscribed on the life. From this point forward the light supplied by the symbol itself must be subordinate; and we must venture at once into that domain of sin and suffering, in which the life of the evil-doer becomes the record of the retributions of the Judge.

But it will deepen our interest in these retributions, and it will at once place the practical purpose of studying them before the mind, if we thus early impress ourselves with the fact, that the subject of them all is MAN. Even when they seem to descend on his dwelling-place, it is at himself they strike. The 'Hand' may write its awful message on the wall, but the writing searches into the soul of the wicked king. The plagues descend on Egypt, but it is Pharaoh and his people who suffer. The history of the retribution may tell us of occurrences in the air, and on the ground, of clouds of locusts, and bloody rivers, and loathsome frogs, and flies, and hail, and thunder, and darkness that might be felt. But through each of these, God was striking at the food, or the joy of human life. The darkness seemed to wrap the land; but it was man that cowered beneath its gloom. The vision of the Sealed Book bears witness to the same fact. Different instruments of retribution are disclosed at the successive opening of the seals; but in every case, these instruments strike at the life of man, or at the accessories of his life. War, pestilence, famine, wild beasts, darkening skies,— each inscribes its message of wrath on the being, the sustenance, or the joy of man.

The book we are studying is therefore the symbol, not merely of a record of judgment, but of the life on which these judgments descend. Whatever can be the symbol of a divine retribution, is a portion of the reality symbolized by this book. Job was referring to it when he lamented that his bones were full of the sins of his youth. David was reading it, when he confessed that his moisture was turned into the drought of summer. Jeremiah's picture of the soul that resembled the heath in the desert, which did not see good when it came; Jude's awful description of human beings who are as clouds without water, and as wandering stars reserved for the blackness of darkness for ever; Paul's account of the men who are given over to delusions to believe a lie; the Saviour's pourtrayal of the Pharisees as graves which men walk over; Isaiah's denunciation of the nation whose root shall be as rottenness, and whose blossom shall go up as the dust; and all the descriptions which the Bible contains of human life, spotted and scarred and torn by sin, are so many quotations and sentences from the book, which is written all over with the inscriptions of doom.

Can we find out in the life, or history of man, where heaven has revealed its wrath against sin? The seven-sealed book was there. It was unsealed for men and angels to read, when fire and brimstone descended upon the inhabitants of Sodom and Gomorrah. The children of Israel beheld one of its seals unloosed, when the dawn disclosed to them the fringe of death, along the border of the Egyptian sea. The sensitive, conscious, responsible life of man is the material of the book. It is human life, in all its developments, in all its circumstances; the human soul; the human body; the life of the home, or the workplace; of the church or the nation. Whatever of man is receptive of retribution,—his affections, hopes, enjoyments, occupations, plans, and convictions,—the entire complex life of humanity in short, as it flows forth, with ceaseless regularity, through the looms of time,—in so far, at least, as it breaks loose from the control of the Great Ruler, and shreds out into self-willed conflict with His laws, or opposition to His cause, or persecution of His people;—this is the surface, the sometimes hidden, sometimes revealed, living, conscious, or unconscious, human surface, on which, from generation to generation, the Lord of providence inscribes His wrath.

When we pass from the consideration of the book to its inscriptions, we have simply to advance one other step, in the study of that same law of retribution, which has led us to the underlying substance of the book itself. If it be the life of the evil-doer, on which God inscribes His wrath, the inscriptions are made by the evil already in the life. What we express by the deepest formula we can use as 'the doom of the Lord,' is, when looked at on another side, the simple consequences of sin. 'Evil pursues the sinner.' Sin cannot exist without consequences. Always it leaves its mark. It writes 'sinner' on the life, or on the portion of the life which has entertained it. Let it only be summoned into existence by any act of man, it is certain to dog that act with confusion, disaster, and shame. Its consequences tell; itself tells. In an infinite variety of ways, it writes its black autographs on the walls of its dwelling-place. And these autographs are the reality symbolized by the inscriptions 'written within and on the back side,' which the Seer beheld, but could not read; the dreary tale of human wickedness and woe inscribed on human life, which expresses even now, and is one day openly to declare, the character and malign destiny of every evil-doer with whom the providence of the Lord has had to deal.

All human life is subject to these inscriptions, and all portions and spheres of life. The illustrations are endless. Take a single faculty and see how it takes on the taint and signature of evil. Take that divinest faculty of our being, the imagination. You can see what it was intended to be in our life, if you examine its first ministries in the life of a child. It is the blessed gift which clothes the common things of earth with celestial light, and imparts the glory and freshness of a dream to everything we see. It turns the plainest home into a palace, and converts the streets of the town we are born in, or the bare heath we go out to play upon, into a wonder world. It opens the gates of the beautiful on every side of us, and takes us, by a thousand avenues, into lands flowing with milk and honey. It is the angel of God leading us up and down the beautiful groves and flower-painted streets of Paradise. It makes the half a greater thing than the whole. Under its teaching, we see a world filled with rainbows, and stars, and brooks, and trees, and lambs frisking on the lea, and birds mounting into the air, and bees gathering honey out of flowers, and the good God and the holy angels walking up and down in the midst of all.

Let the possessor of this divine faculty pass under the yoke of an impure or worldly passion. The imagination does not cease to work, but its direction is changed. It opens the doorways of heaven no more—no more introduces the soul to the company of angels. It becomes the handmaid of the evil passion—goes out into foul places—brings back pictures and visions of vileness, vile thoughts and vile songs, and opens up a whole world of evil, closed to the pure soul. That which was sent to be an angel of God in the soul, becomes a hewer of wood and a drawer of water in the lowest and foulest levels of life.

Take a single victim of sin apart, and examine him narrowly. Let him be one who is leading a licentious life. Look into his eyes, his face, his personal form and bearing. It may be years before he shall be summoned to his final doom; yet he is already a parchment written over with divine retribution. Within and without, over all his being, thousands of intersecting spots and lines tell the same story. His eyes are bloodshot; his skin is shrivelled; his bones are rotten; his lungs are diseased; his brain is on fire, or the fire is burnt out, and a palsy is trickling down his nerves; wrinkles, which the eye cannot see, syllable his life on all the tissues of his body; and in eye and ear, in heart and limb, aches and spasms and impotences, which pass for other things, illustrate the handwriting of evil, and tell to those who know the language, as plainly as if it were written in English characters, that this is a man who is living under the doom of the Lord.

It is the same with social wickedness. Long before the last shock of judgment falls, the retribution has begun to descend. Like a poison in the air, or a pestilence in a city, the evil which belongs to a community shows itself by a trail of judgments. It kills out truth, or nobleness, or purity, or reverence from the national character. It puts its mark, like some death-spot, upon the face of the community. Look at any social wrong, at human slavery, for example, and suppose it folded up among the institutions of any—the strongest and greatest nation upon earth. It will inscribe its name on the life of that nation. Put a gag in its mouth, that it may not speak; put chains upon its feet, that it may not break loose; hide it in swamps, where its cry will not be heard; or, treating it tenderly, swaddle it in bodily comforts, that its degradation may be forgotten. Put down all cruel treatment of it. Banish the whipping-post and the lash. Keep the slave-market well in the background. Repudiate the slave-ship. Would you then succeed in preventing, or effacing the marks of the iniquity? No; it would reveal itself in the laws and acts of the nation, in the life and character of the citizens, in the looks and habits, the language and bearing of every child in the land. The very appearance of the country would tell that the earth had been cursed on its account.[1]

[1] 'The climate in Georgia,' wrote an intelligent traveller through the Slave States of America, before these States had taken on the more frightful imprints of the war, 'is fine, the country is more salubrious. Why, then, is she left behind in the race of development and prosperity? I can see no reason except the ever-recurring one—Slavery! . . . . . In Illinois (where there are no slaves) all was life, and hope, and eagerness; *here*, a dull stagnation prevails. In Illinois the cars were crowded with emigrants, or speculators, or men anxiously looking for new homes. At every station a new city, at lowest a new town or village, was springing up; and on every hand the click of the hammer and the rasping of the saw betokened that new inhabitants had pitched their tents in the land of promise. In Georgia how different! . . . There is none of that bustle or hopeful eagerness. You travel for a hundred miles, and see no village; and not unfrequently you pass lands where the young green pines tell you that abandoned fields are returning to their primeval wildness.'—*Stirling's Letters from the Slave States.*

It has become common to point to the late war in America, between the North and the South, and say, 'Behold God's judgment upon slavery.' But that judgment did not wait for that terrible war to announce its presence. The darkening of the moral sense in relation to the slave; the almost universal hardening of the conscience against his sufferings and his natural human rights; the blotting out of the instincts of humanity when kinship with the slave was asserted; the scorn and loathing of the divine image in coloured skin, which were so common among the upholders of slavery; and the cruel practices to which slavery led; and the unjust laws which were passed to protect it; and the proud resentment, by all classes, of counsel or warning from without :—these were the direct unfoldings of the iniquity, the handwriting of the nation's crime on every surface of its life.

The late Isaac Taylor sometimes diverged into the fields of historical illustration, with a success which suggests, what a historical illustration of retribution, imperfect though the materials are, might have become in such hands. Read this short passage from his *Saturday Evening*. It illustrates Christ's inscription of wrath on the life of the Church :—

'While the Church was one, Christianity spread; or, should we not say, burst over the world, gathering myriads of converts from lands within and far beyond the limits of the Roman empire. When Christians became factious, and when other names than the name Christ were called upon, then the evangelical circle drew in apace : no more conquests were made, or they were conquests purely nominal; and ere long the fierce avenger of the Lord's quarrel with His Church, breaking bounds, sword in hand, from his sultry Arabian sands, drove the distracted flock from field to field, until the

Christian name was near to be quite lost from the world.' . . . 'In the course of a thousand years scarcely a single light was carried (by the Church of the middle ages) into the centre of the gross darkness that covered the earth; or if carried, was soon extinguished. Should we learn nothing from the contemplation of such a course of events? Shall we fear nothing when we have proof before us, that the principles of the divine government actually admit of the long-continued, and almost total, withdrawal of efficacious influence from the Church? Shall we take no warning when a lesson like this is drawn out at large in our view, and we see that the Lord adheres to a system of PUBLIC RETRIBUTION in His conduct towards His people as a body; and that, when they refuse to hearken to His voice in capital matters, He retires as if in grief to the recesses of the invisible state, and though He preserves the spark of piety on earth from extinction, will do no more? Thus was it in fact from the sixth to the sixteenth century.'

As with nations and churches, so with races of men. The white man, pressing along the path of his destiny, finds on every shore he colonizes, aboriginal races who retire, as he advances, into the interior of their land. Every year diminishes their power of resistance and their numbers. What trifling it is to say, in explanation, that they have smaller brains, or a weaker organization, or they have failed to draw into the blood of their race the ingredients of strength which give the battle to us! *Why* did they fail to mix with nobler blood? *What* weakened their organization, or made their brains small? Retrace their history. Study their traditions, their speech, their habits, their very countenances. These tell of other days, and of far other conditions of life. You are carried back beyond the stages depicted by Paul, back to piety, vigour, national splendour in some distant age, perhaps in some far-off clime. You see by the very relics of the past in their possession, that they were once, as we are now, the stewards and vessels of civilisation. And you also see, that, like the nations driven out by Israel, and like Israel itself in later days, they were untrue to their stewardship, untrue to the position and duty assigned them by God, and are now in consequence wasting away. 'The heathen are sunk down in the pit they have made.' Their feebleness is retribution. When the path to heaven was open to their ancestors, they despised it. They trod the elements of permanent well-being beneath their feet. Law and righteousness, truth and purity, they cast from them as worthless things. They put eternity and love and humanity out of their sight. They did not care to keep the old faith in a righteous Judge in their hearts. By their evil deeds, they suffered to be blotted out the handwriting of this Judge from their consciences. In short, they forgot God and followed after idols, and became a nation of evil-doers; and then, in the lapse of generations,—by the decree of Him who visits the iniquity of the fathers upon the children,—a broken, disunited, and feeble race. And now, in the destruction they are undergoing, they are, by the same decree, being turned into that 'hell' that awaits the nations who forget God.[1] This destruction? It is the handwriting of their sin upon their life.

But individual instances, culled in this way here and there, can give but a meagre view of that universal and unending process, by which the entire bypast life of humanity, has been written over with the handwriting of sin and judgment. To fill up a proper illustration, would

[1] Ps. ix. 17, 'The wicked shall be turned into hell, and all the nations that forget God.'

be to write the history of our race. Only historical instances, and those drawn from the widest reaches of history, could adequately display the number and character, the fulness and tragic compressure, of those inscriptions which crowd this book. But history, like the men who write it, must be born again before it can serve the Lord Christ, or illustrate the acts of His government. Hitherto it has been a glorifier, not of God, but of man. It has supplied us with the court registers and battle almanacs of the past; the real conflict of the ages, the story of man's master relationship, it only here and there, and in briefest snatches, attempts to tell. Yet if history did lie open to us, as one day doubtless it shall lie; and if the true record of the past, as the Divine Historian knows it, were liberated from the oblivion, in which it is at present imbedded; and the actual shape and features, and the real beginnings and endings, of the human story were laid bare,—we might open at any page, and find illustrations in the life and history of any generation. But seals are on the book. We hardly know the past. Death, and oblivion, and man's forgetfulness, hide it from our view.[1] Imagine an ancient manuscript, written in extinct characters, frayed away at the edges, the writing blotted out along the

---

[1] 'Time sadly overcometh all things, and is now dominant, and sitteth on a sphinx, and looketh unto Memphis and old Thebes; while his sister Oblivion reclineth semi-somnous on a pyramid, gloriously triumphing, making puzzles of Titanian erections, and turning old glories into dreams. History sinketh beneath her cloud. The traveller, as he paceth amazedly through those deserts, asketh of her, Who built them? And she mumbleth something, but what it is he knoweth not.'—SIR THOMAS BROWNE.

margins, and only a little stream of unconnected words, saved from each line, running down the centre of the page. Such is our knowledge of the past. We have to decipher the characters, and spell out the meaning, of the missing and existing words as best we may. Yet it is wonderful, how true even these fragments are to the fact, that the past is a surface written over with autographs of judgment. Imperfectly as we know the history of those who have preceded us on the earth, it is obviously the history of a conflict between good and evil. And from Cain to the men who crucified our Lord, that history tells of thwarted efforts to crush out goodness and truth from the earth. Every page, however dimly as yet to our eyes, bears the impress of man's iniquity and God's revenge. We only require to name over the successive representatives of the world-power which have occupied the field of time, to summon witnesses of this fact. Babel and Egypt, Assyria and Babylon, and Rome, each in its turn, and in its own way, set itself against the truth and people of God. In their pride of self-worship, they would tread out the fire from heaven. And the fire kindled on them and consumed them. One by one, those proud embodiments of the worldly principle were left smouldering in their own ashes.

> 'The breath of heaven has blown away
>   What toiling earth had piled;
> Scattering wise heart and crafty hand,
> As breezes strew on ocean's sand,
>   The fabrics of a child.
> Divided thence through every age,
> Thy rebels, Lord, their warfare wage;
>   And hoarse and jarring all

> Mount up their heaven-assailing cries,
> To Thy bright watchmen in the skies,
> From Babel's shattered wall.'[1]

In all the past, nothing has prospered, nothing has planted itself permanently on the earth, which 'set itself against the Lord and His Anointed,' or tried to suppress His truth. Even under the haze and dimness of the earliest ages, we can still see, that in the end evil slew the wicked; that some Cain-mark, or mark of the beast, was impressed on the current wickedness of the times; and that, in one form or other, the judgments of the Lord upon evil-doing have been abroad in every generation.

The researches of those who labour among the *debris* of the past, land us at the same conclusion. A traveller alights on a sand-waste. The memorials of other days are concealed beneath his feet. He digs. A buried city answers to his toil. Artists and thinkers pause beside the carved heads of bulls, and winged creatures, and unnamed kings, which this city discloses to their view. Those paintings still fresh on walls which have not been gazed on for two thousand years, tell of life and toil, of wealth and pomp, of art and intellect, of ambition and conflict, in times and circles far removed from our own. But they tell of other things more surely still. From sculptured stone and painted wall, comes up the story of a nation which knew not God. This is Nineveh, when Jonah's words were forgotten. In the soul of the spectator, the chariots of her pride are once more whirling along those gorgeous streets. The crowned riders, the

[1] *The Christian Year.*

prancing horses, the noise of the whips, the gleaming of the cruel swords, the glittering of the spears which drank the blood of the innocent, the multitude of the slain,[1] and all the sad and pitiful tokens of a national life which rejected God, come crowding into his thoughts. But he emerges from the excavations. Around him is a waste. Birds of ill omen are wheeling about the solitude. The wild beast has made its lair among the topmost ruins. The handwriting of the Judge is there.

It is the language of every similar ruin. If from a proper vantage-spot, we could survey the scenes which man has occupied in the past; if we could go high enough, to look down upon the ruins and memorial places he has left behind, the field of our vision would be crowded with lines and interlines, or say rather, with the illuminated borders, of the story of retribution. That waste in the distance, which the wild creatures of the swamps and the woods are reclaiming to their use, was a country which poured out its life in ambitious wars. That nearer solitude contains the ruins of churches which were unfaithful to the truth. Fleets of merchantmen once rode in those waters which, through national dishonesty, are shallow and deserted now. The stones which rise amid those sands are the pillars and doorways of temples, whose worship was too impure to continue. And these and all similar remains of human activity—Gizeh-pyramids, Elephanta-caves, Sphinxes, Baalbecs, and Carnacs—mere dots and deeper markings of a text too scant to pourtray the past,—footprints of extinct creatures on the upper crust of the earth—bear witness to buried

[1] *Vid.* Nahum iii.

lines and chapters of that story which crowds the seven-sealed book.[1]

But it is nearer home, in our domestic memories and amid the graves of our kindred, that we find the last and most impressive illustration of the things written in the seven-sealed book. The inscriptions of retribution run over mysteriously upon the margins of our most tender sorrows. I take you to a little grave in the family burying-place. You think of the sweet face, all soiled now, put out of view there. Your heart goes faster as you recall the joys which centred in the dear one sleeping

---

[1] 'An hour more brought us in sight of Delphi—once the richest oracular site in the world; a city of temples, statues, hippodromes, theatres, votive offerings of the costliest works of art, gold and silver, precious stones, from far and near, from Greek and barbarian; city of song and dance, and Pythian games, and solemn deputations from Athens, from Corinth, from every other renowned city upon the earth. These terraces were once covered with the most magnificent temples—above them all, the hippodrome or stadium. The natural form remains; the terraces, with huge masses of masonry here and there, exist still. Two or three wretched monasteries, as many churches, like hovels; a narrow, muddy street or two; rows of tile-roofed dirty huts, bits of hewn marble built into rude walls, fragments of exquisite sculpture turned topsy-turvy and stuck into enclosures; foundation-stones, covered with inscriptions still legible, and telling the splendid story of other times;—these are the Delphi of to-day. To stand here and think that in Homer's time the temple of Delphi was reverenced beyond the limits of the Grecian name; to recall its increasing splendours for a thousand years, and the immense influence it exercised through the whole period of ancient history; and to look at it now, and see, as we saw to-day, half-a-dozen barefooted Delphian maids washing clothes in the basin supplied by the Castalian spring, in the midst of the annihilation of so much splendour—we can hardly call it ruin—is a solemn spectacle of the vanity and perishableness of all human grandeur.'

below. Perhaps you think of the sufferings which hastened on the end, and of the sharp wrenches of agony in yourself when the end did come; but, besides all this, there is a dumb, uneasy feeling, a shapeless consciousness of something somewhere wrong, which was the far-back cause of your bereavement, which you seldom pause to interpret to yourself, but which is yet the working of a hidden sense of the divine justice which dominates over the life of man. Dumb and shapeless though this feeling be, it points to a great deep in God's dealings with our race. It is the echo in our spirits, of the judgments of the past.—' Death by sin!'—If sin had not entered the world, neither would you be weeping over that little mound of earth.[1] The mystery which that grave covers is part of the book which Christ holds in His hand, which only He has prevailed to open, and which is written within and without. By this small grave we may pass inward among the retributions of the past. Into what a world it has admitted us! The congregation of the dead are here. Here lie the ashes of the generations which preceded our own. Our fathers and mothers sleep under the soil we tread. If you dig, you may bring up the clay of the first of your name. The very dust the wind whirls in eddies from your feet, ' may have been worshipped once in the faces of forgotten kings.' The very graveyards themselves go to decay. Where old towns and

---

[1] 'Death is as much the natural consequence of sin, as it is the penalty of sin. It forms the termination of an historical process by a law that regulates the succession of events, as well as the termination of a judicial process under the power and authority of a lawgiver.'—*Chalmers' Com.* Rom. viii. 2.

villages buried their dead, the corn and the barley of living populations wave. The earth is one vast sepulchre. It is all filled in this way, with the judicial glory of the Judge.[1] On hill and vale, by stream and sea, it is all dug over with graves. All the generations which ever sweated on its surface are at rest under its coverlid of green. An innumerable multitude of all times and kindreds are sleeping the long sleep in the great mother's breast. And at this moment thousands of all tongues and countries are descending into the same repose. It is a repose which conceals the handwriting of this judgment-book. Over all this territory, on which death sits in such gloomy potency—along all those lines of human life, which terminate so inexorably in the grave—in the graves of generations, and nations, and families—in every remotest, quietest resting-place of the dead, the stern autographs of judgment are disclosed, and the old words of the prophet, with a time-wide breadth of application, are sounded forth: 'They that depart from me shall be *written in the earth.*'

[1] See Num. xiv. 21–23, and Isa. vi. 3, where the 'glory' is plainly that of retribution.

IV.

SEALS.

'The Lord does not come once merely with clouds at the end of the world, but through all periods of the world's history. Where the carcase is, there the eagles are gathered together. The truth that the Lord comes with clouds, renews itself with every oppression of the Church by the world.'—HENGSTENBERG.

IT has been usual with those who have undertaken a demonstration of the final judgment, to argue from the present inequality of rewards and punishments. The circumstances of human life, it is said, are such, that those who deserve most highly are least rewarded, and the least deserving receive the crowns. It is Nero who is robed in purple: to Paul is assigned a chain. Before these inequalities could be rectified here, the good and the bad are alike removed from the scene. Even when the wicked survive to encounter punishment for their misdeeds, they seldom receive a full retribution. And if, now and again, the righteous have prosperity, either it is not up to the height of the services they have rendered, or it arises from some accidental cause. In the interests of justice, a day is owing in which these anomalies may be corrected.

The argument must be allowed. But it will be good to guard our minds against a tendency with which it is unconsciously charged. It is the tendency to limit the domain of retribution; to project the mind unduly into the future, and shut our eyes to the judgments of the present and the past. God does not postpone to the close of the world the distribution of His judicial awards. Only the declaration of the distribution is postponed. The last day is a Day of Manifestation. The hidden things are to be brought to light on that day. But in every generation, judgments are abroad upon the earth. The area of retribution is the history of the race. Judgment began when the curse first fell on our world. From that hour to this it has never intermitted. The events of human history are the embodied sentences of the Judge. In the divine government, the exercise of judgment is as constant as that of mercy and truth.

The history of man is the evolution of concurrent and successive cycles, which close with judgment. A time of probation is followed by a time of judgment. The old world had its judgment-day at the deluge; the world of Sodom and Gomorrah, on that awful night when Lot and his daughters were led forth by the angels. The judgment-day for Pharaoh was when he entered the channels of the Red Sea; and for the Jewish nation, when Jerusalem was destroyed by Rome. The future judgment is the close of the greatest cycle of all.

The future judgment is the most awful of these manifestations of divine wrath, because it is the last. It is wider and more universal in its sweep than the others. It is also the formal revelation and announcement—the conclusion and summing up—of all the judgments which have gone before. But it is only the widest and last of an ascending series. The judgments which precede it are acts of the same administration, and exhibitions of the same divine anger against sin. They are the successive shocks of an earthquake which is to culminate in the destruction of the world. Each shock, as it comes, is a prelusion of the last. As it was in the days of Noah and of Lot, so it will be in the days which terminate the world. As the type prefigures the antitype, as the twilight foreshadows the night, so those past and concurrent retributions of Providence, at the close of cycles of probation, announce and herald the last dread day of doom. They are its forerunners and premonitions—the shadows, lengthening as the day draws near, of the great white throne ; and they are allowed and revealed in mercy, to quicken the conscience of the race, and train it to an expectation and healthy awe of that day.

But these prelusive judgments are little known. The book is sealed with seals. We do not see its contents, or we do not see them as what they are. The retributions it reveals, are not known as retributions. Our knowledge at the best is limited, our insight dim and poor, and the 'thoughts' of the Judge 'are very deep.' Time, and place, and life, and death, and early training, and the habits of later years, and sense, and sin, and man's forgetfulness, and a thousand other things, conceal them from our view. It is only at rare intervals, and by the eyes of a very few, that even glimpses of such facts are seen. The 'secret of the Lord is with them that fear Him,' and with them only in their highest moods. To the most of men, providence is a mere mirror, in which the confused opinions and dubious actions of the race are reflected.

'God's judgments are far above out of their sight.' 'They are seated on the brim of the ocean of existence; but they do not penetrate into its depths: they march along the sea, and behold only a little of the foam which the waves cast upon the shore.'[1]

The habit of expecting from the future what is already by our side, is one cause of our blindness to the retributions of the present. We underrate the present, and are surprised when it brings a judgment to our door. Yet if we cast our eyes backward over the best known portions of the past, and see how every succeeding age brought to its termination some scheme or institution, some government, law, or nation, which had been on its trial up till then, which had grown and become corrupt, and was ready to perish, it ought to be no surprise to us to discover, that similar issues are taking place at present. Every age, I might say every day, is a judgment-day. 'Every morning doth He bring judgment to light.' Even while I write these words, the term of probation for some life or scheme, or institution, or nation, is coming to a close. At this very moment, the trumpet is sounding, and the angels are gathering for the fire, 'the wood, and the hay, and the stubble,' and also, alas, the men who used them; and judgment is passing forth on unrighteous attempts to build up the edifice of life, in neglect or scorn of God. Who is not aware that the French Revolution at the close of the last century was a most real judgment-day for those who were submerged in it? Was the shaking of European thrones and nations, over all the Continent in 1848, anything short of

[1] De Lamennais: *Words of a Believer*.

a 'crack of doom?' And surely, without stepping beyond the present hour, I may assert, that the air we breathe is at this moment pealing with the doom of wicked institutions and tyrannical governments, in opposite regions of the earth. The very ground we tread, if we had the ears to hear, is resonant with the chariot-wheels of approaching retribution. In a thousand directions 'the Judge is at the door.' Over a thousand spheres of action, the judgment hour is striking. Judgments are abroad on the paths we frequent, but we take no heed. The earth, the air, the lives and homes of men, are full of retribution; but they come and go, and leave no footprint on our hearts.

Our subjection to sense, and the consequent tendency to judge according to appearance, is another cause of the dimness which seems to lie on the world of retribution. The apparent prosperity of the wicked is a standing difficulty with the people of God. They see despisers and evil-doers prospering in their way, and flourishing like green bay trees, and they ask, ' Have we cleansed our hearts in vain? Is there not a Judge who doeth right?' When the Lord's people put such questions, they are judging His acts hastily, and according to appearance; they are basing their judgment on the facts which strike the outward eye alone. And a judgment so built up is sure to be wrong. 'Appearance' is no mark of well-being in the sphere of Providence. The prosperity which visits the despiser of the cross, is far more frequently the sign of a reality in God, than in him who receives it. It is the new and added gush of paternal goodness, to lead the poor sinner to repentance. And when it is not that, when it is a sign of the sinner's own condition, it is simply his perilous elevation to the height from which God is preparing to cast him down. In all circumstances it is a temporary, transitory gift. All the while of it, the Lord is angry with the unbelief of its possessor. All the while of it, He is writing down wrath against him for the day of wrath. All the while of it, His face is set against him and his plans. And the man's want of real peace, his discontent and restless striving, his sense of emptiness, and longing for some other good than he possesses, are the terrible proofs within his own being, that there is a Judge in the earth who doeth righteously.

A third cause of our blindness to such events, is the foregone conclusion, that retribution is only present when *the last results* of sin have been reached. But it is not merely as coinciding with the terminations of long-continued iniquity, that the present may be the scene of divine retribution. Numerous though the final issues of evil in nations or individuals must be in any age, they are but a small portion of the judgments actually coming forth upon sin. Every step in the history of sin is a step into the domain of retribution. 'Can one go upon hot coals, and his feet not be burned?' Judgment manifests itself in the partial as well as in the complete developments of evil.

A fourth cause which seals up the prelusive judgments from our view, is the mistaken conceptions of retribution which we entertain. We are wrong in our notions of its nature and manifestations. Even when retributions are present and palpable to the senses, we will not believe them to be outbreakings of the divine wrath on sin. We suffer ourselves to be blinded by phrases which hide out the truth. We say—we think we have explained them when we say—they are the accidents of circumstances, or the natural fruits of evil. We do not see that there can be no such accidents. We do not sufficiently remember, that the natural fruits of evil are themselves a doom. We insist on extraneous and formal dooms. Retribution must come forth clad in miraculous and visible garments. It must be a handwriting on the wall, a portent in the heavens, a sounding of trumpets in the sky. But this is merely the aberration of our ignorance. Retribution can only on rare occasions be clothed in formalities like these. Its manifestations, for the most part, and of necessity, are not miraculous, but natural. It is at work when we, who are in its presence, see only decay, or disease, or accident. It comes forth as the destroying powers in nature do,—sometimes indeed in terrible and fiery splendours, but oftenest in utter quietness; quietly, stealthily, unannounced, like mildew or blight, like disease or death. It makes no noise, proclaims no miracle, but enters not the less surely, the life, or home, or country which it has been commissioned to inscribe with the sentences of the Judge.

Let us suppose ourselves living in the earliest times of the Christian faith. We shall take our places for a little among the first disciples and apostles of the Lord, and make their age our own. When we look out upon the world they have been summoned to subdue, two horizons appear girdling the scene. Within the nearest lies the Jewish, beyond that and within the remote horizon, the Gentile world. If we examine the life which these horizons enclose, and think of the bitter hatred of Jew and Gentile to the truth, the doom which each had drawn down upon itself can hardly fail to suggest itself to our minds. But, thinking of that doom, with our knowledge of what was still future to them, the likelihood is, that our thoughts would run forward to Titus and his Roman legions beleaguering Jerusalem, and to the decline and fall of the Roman Empire. And most certainly, retribution was present in these catastrophes. But it was not poured out then for the first time, nor then more really, than when the disciples and apostles began their career.

Stand beside Jesus and His disciples as they are descending Olivet. Survey the city over whose doom the tears of the Redeemer have been shed. A magnificence unequalled in the past is displayed in every street. A temple more glorious than Solomon's adorns the sacred hill. The very fishermen of Galilee are attracted by 'its goodly stones.' Yet the angels of judgment are on the scene. What has forced the tears from Christ? Titus and his cohorts are not in sight for a generation to come. A vision of the beleaguered city is indeed present among His thoughts; but not that alone. A retribution nearer and more searching is descending even while He weeps. He weeps because it is descending. On all that city's life is crushing down, sore and heavy, the sevenfold woe on existing sin![1] The Lord sees a people without a shepherd, a temple without faith, a nation without life. A career which might have been glorious is going down in clouds. The life of the nation is tarnished. The purpose of its existence is frustrated. Spiritual death is reigning where life should have been. Falsehood and hol-

[1] Matt. xxiii. 13-23.

lowness, and avarice and cruelty, are the ruling principles of individual life. The teachers and guides of the people have become whited sepulchres, and their teaching has come to have the miserable result of making the disciple twofold more a 'child of hell' than the teacher himself.

When we pass the horizon which enclosed Jewish life, and step out upon the wider field of Paganism, we find ourselves at once in the presence of retributive forces actively at work. Suppose a quarter of a century to have passed since the tears over Jerusalem were shed. Transport yourselves to Corinth, and enter the room where Paul is dictating his epistle to the Christians at Rome. The introductory sentences are already penned. He has announced the subject of the epistle. He is about to give forth his awful description of the heathen half of that world which the gospel was given to reclaim. He begins by stating, that 'the wrath of God is revealed from heaven against all ungodliness and unrighteousness of men.' The statement carries in its first impression the announcement of some formal doom. It is 'wrath of God,' and it is 'wrath revealed from heaven,'—a revelation of wrath. But the profound teaching of the apostle is, that the ungodliness and unrighteousness are themselves a main portion of the doom. That catalogue of human misconduct, so dark with the shadows of depravity, so loaded with treason to human nature and God, revealing at every link infidelity to some sacred tie, —this is itself 'the wrath,' the handwriting of the Judge, 'revealed from heaven.' Wrath lies upon all ungodliness and unrighteousness of men: behold the wrath in their lives! A curse descends on all who forsake God:

behold the curse in their very farness from God! Destruction waits on those who worship idols: behold the destruction in the natural fruits of their idolatry! They corrupted their conceptions of God, and became corrupt in consequence themselves. In the service of their vile gods, the very affections of their nature became vile; and hell was already kindled within them, in their foul and unnatural desires. So careful is the apostle to impress his readers with this view of retribution, that he gives the progression of the judgment. As he proceeds with his description, you can trace the judgment descending by slow but certain stages, from deep to deep, and towards the lowest deep, carrying its poor victims in its arms. It is virtually a history of spiritual and social deterioration: first, there is a people instructed and spiritual, standing in the presence of the glories of the universe; then, there is the descent of this instructed people into neglect of spiritual duties. 'When they knew God, they glorified Him not AS GOD, neither were thankful.' Then, there is spiritual darkness arising out of this negligence. Then, on the darkness, there is self-erection,—self-worship,—folly. Then, by this folly, there is bartering away of the truth for falsehood,—'the exchanging of the glory of the uncorruptible God for an image made like to corruptible man, and four-footed beasts, and creeping things.' Then, there is licentiousness in the life; then, faith in the falsehoods on which such life was built; and, last of all, utter ungodliness, inhumanity, and moral and social ruin.

If these causes bedim the inscriptions of judgment

which are being entered on the living page of the Present, THE FUTURE totally conceals them. We only see in part. Life is short, and retribution is long. 'The mills of God,' although they grind surely, 'grind slowly.' And only a short reach of any retributive process may be unfolded, in the days of those who suffered from the crimes which brought it down. To all that lies in the future, we are totally blind. God may be inscribing His wrath upon His enemies, but His handwriting is as yet concealed. The judgments may be travelling onwards, but their path is in the deep. They lurk in the habits or deeds of the people on whom they are to descend, but only as seeds of wrath. No appearance of retribution darkens the sky under which the iniquities are wrought. Even the near future is dark to us. The Pharaoh is still lord; his cruel edicts are still law; his throne is firm; his chariots and horsemen come forth at his beck. It is only God who sees the angel of the pestilence in the distance, and hears the rushing of the returning waves on horse and rider in the Red Sea. The Jezebel winds her wicked wiles around innocent Naboth, and transfers the vineyard to her husband; but the dogs which are to eat her flesh, under the walls of her palace, are only visible to God. The Herod is all-powerful at Cesarea: prisons open and shut, swords wave and heads fall off, at his bidding; the air is filled with the noise of his flatterers; but the worms which are lurking in their holes at to-morrow's gate, with God's commission to destroy him, no human eye can see.

In the presence of facts like these, we are compelled to acknowledge the immense distance which separates our knowledge of retribution from God's. With Him there is absolute knowledge of it all. From end to end, there is 'no darkness nor shadow of death, where the workers of iniquity may hide themselves' from their doom. Doom and doomed, past and to come, are continually beneath His eye. The past is an open book to Him. The future is as the past. The thousand years which form an impenetrable veil to us, to Him are 'as yesterday when it is past.' There is no past, no future, but an everlasting Now. 'He seeth the end from the beginning.' What we name future is all in His hands, and written over with His decrees. Dark to us, it is clear as sunlight to Him.

If men could see and believe this, there might be no need of revelation such as John records. But the wicked scoff at it, and the eyes of the righteous are dim.

To the wicked themselves, this blankness of the future is itself a portion of their doom. It is surcharged with wrath for them, and they will not believe that wrath is there. There is fatal calm, fatal peace, fatal appearance of prosperity, at the very moment they are standing on the brink of ruin. The past brings no monition to their hearts. It is an old tale, the fable of an old world, in the estimate of their philosophy. If God ever did drown a world for its ungodliness, or rain down fire from heaven, it was in another world than ours; or it is long, long past, and it cannot occur again. We are in new epochs now, under surer laws now. Miraculous fires and floods are dead and buried. 'And all things continue as they were from the beginning of the world.' And so the scoffers scoff, 'walking after their own lusts, and saying, Where is the promise of His coming?'

Even for the righteous, there is no escape from perplexity but by faith. The seal of the future is as impervious to them as to the wicked, if they neglect to exercise their faith. At all critical periods in the history of God's people, the darkness of the future has been a trial to their souls. Standing on the border of an untrodden territory, on whose minutest landmarks the most absolute darkness rests, they have oftentimes been perplexed. The visible, palpable, material present surrounded them with its phenomena, and they, too, have been tempted to say, 'All things shall continue as they were.'

Inspired prophets, gazing into the future with the divine eyes, can see afar the handwriting of the Judge on every manifestation of iniquity. But inspired insight is rare. For the most part, God's people occupy the present in sorrow. They are in the midst of the 'perpetual desolations.' They hear the roaring of the enemies in the midst of the congregation. They do not see 'the signs' of the divine presence. The seals are on the book. It would be life to them to know that judgment is preparing for their enemies, and they do not know it. The book is closed and sealed with seals, and the eye of man cannot read what is written on its page.

These feelings repeat themselves in every crisis of the Church. Ever there is an hour of darkness before the dawn, a time when the hearts of the godly cry, 'How long, O Lord, how long?' The future rises up thick with clouds, or descends like a fog of death on the pathway of the truth. The seals reappear on the book. The little handful of believing hearts, who began to breathe out their sighs and longings, in the bosom of the Papal Church in the fifteenth century, were in circumstances not unlike those of the early Christians. It was still Rome which persecuted them; but it was a Rome more cruel, more wicked, more corrupt, than the Rome of Domitian and Nero. Popes and inquisitions, papal kings and armies, chains, and dungeons, and fagots, stood heaped up in the way of the truth, and dared it to advance. The Wycliffe, the Luther, the Calvin, the Knox —the strong arms of the Reformation who were one day to strike down the Papacy—are still far in the distance, and unseen. The seals are on the book. Here and there, indeed, along the path, a clear-eyed martyr gazing from the scaffold or the stake, could see the judgments and the splendours behind the veil. Huss, quivering under the arrow which struck himself, beheld the heavens filled with eagles hastening to prey on the carcase of his destroyers; and brave Hugh Latimer at the stake, before Balliol College in Oxford, could say to his companion in tribulation, 'Be of good comfort, Master Ridley, and play the man. We shall this day light such a candle, by God's grace, in England, as, I trust, shall never be put out.' But glances like these were uncommon. The persecuted had little hope for the world. The world, by their reckoning, was near its end. And if they did not lose heart for themselves, it was because they looked above the darkness, and knew that personal deliverance was not far away. Through the fires of persecution and martyrdom, was a short pass into the joys and liberty of heaven. They left a world bereft of justice for a heaven where it was supreme. 'Farewell sun, moon, and stars,' said the Covenanter M'Kail, 'farewell weak and frail body; farewell father and mother; farewell green earth and happy home! and welcome eternity, welcome angels and saints, welcome Christ the Saviour of the world, and welcome God the Judge of all.' But what sorrow is in these words! They are the words of one to whom the future here is dark. His appeal is to the heavens —the just God is there. For his poor country and the world there is nothing but woe. The seals are on the book.

And to-day it is as in these days gone by. God holds the future in His own hand as closely now as then. The minutest fragment of it baffles our most piercing scrutiny. We cannot tell what a day will bring forth. Did any prophet disclose, at the beginning of last year, the events which marked its course? Can the wisest foresee, what is to take place before the close of the present year? For us, as for the early Christians and the Reformers, the seals are on the book.

And yet it seems to me, as if our lot had fallen on a time not less momentous, in respect of its issues, than any past time, except one, which could be named. We are evidently on the brink of such changes as the world has never yet seen. Our age is an age of upbreaking and awakening, and conflict. Everything is on trial. The principles embodied for ages in human institutions have stepped forth unclothed, to try their strength for the future empire of the world. Convictions, churches, governments, laws: they are all stripped for the fight; and —as if to proffer their services to the successful wrestlers, —those new elements of human power, those gigantic forces, of which our fathers did not dream, which have come to us from fire, and air, and water, and have such power to shape and reshape the habits of civilised existence, seem waiting on the issue. The conflict is still the old and hoary battle between good and evil. On the one side in this conflict, stands up to wrestle for the dominion, the same wicked, godless, unrepenting world which crucified our Lord, and put apostles, and confessors, and reformers, and Scottish covenanters to death; and, notwithstanding all that Christianity has wrought, there is still on that side in the conflict, a certain serious amount of cupidity in commerce, and insolence in authority, and crookedness in state policy, and hurtfulness in social customs, and the hard face and glazed eye of unbelief of spiritual truth. Things, too, which we had begun to fancy were growing old, and ready to vanish away, have put on new strength for the battle. Oppressors of nations are still, in many parts of the earth, powerful on their thrones. Defrauders of workmen are still fattening on the hire they have withholden, and vindicating their wickedness by glozing words. The barbarous war-spirit is as strong, and active, and insolent as ever. State-bound churches are still in existence. Even the slave-trade, the most fiendish misuse of commerce ever perpetrated on the earth, is abroad, and more vigorous than ever. In a single year recently on the seaboard of Africa, nineteen thousand human beings were hunted like wild beasts, and torn from their homes to be sold as slaves. Entire tribes of the African race are vanishing from the land of their fathers. And travellers in many days' journeys find nothing but ruined villages and towns.[1]

Sanguine hearts look wistfully to this and the other favoured spot, to this and the other nook, where the evil-doer is on the losing side. They seem to themselves to see in these, the beginnings of the Nemesis. But it is in mere corners of the world where these streaks of hope are seen. If we would see the world as it actually is, we must include continents in our survey,—all Europe, all

---

[1] 'The tribes which formerly furnished most of the slaves are now nearly extinct, and the country between the coast and the Lake Nyassa is fast becoming depopulated. An Arab merchant, who recently returned here from Nyassa, informed me that he travelled for seventeen days through a country covered with ruined towns and villages, which a few years ago were inhabited by the M'Nyassa and Mizzahow tribes, and where now no living soul is seen. Last year 19,000 slaves were imported through the Custom-house here; of these, 4000 were from the coast opposite, and 15,000 from Keelwa, and destination of the caravans from the Nyassa. Every year the slave traffic is extended further into the interior.'—*Extract of a Letter from the Consul at Zanzibar to his Excellency Sir George Grey. Aug.* 1860.

'The slave-hunting system has come across our path, and has nearly quite depopulated the valley of the lower Shire. You may have heard that certain slave-dealers came along Dr Kirk's path, from Tette to this river, instigated one tribe against another, and were paid in captives, some of whom we liberated. A panic seized the population of a large district above the cataracts. They fled to the Shire, leaving their fine gardens and grain behind them; a drought and famine followed—thousands perished, and still die off daily. We counted thirty-two dead bodies floating down as we steamed up; and these are nothing to those who perish in the villages and lie unburied, or those that pass by at night, or are devoured by alligators.'—*Letter from Dr Livingstone to Mr Wm. Logan, Glasgow. Feb.* 1863.

Asia, Africa, America, the whole earth. The outpouring of retribution, on here and there a spot, where evil has been triumphant, is but a drop on a world, whose parched lips are gasping for vengeance in every clime. Lift up your eyes, I pray you, and from this green nook in England, where Sabbath bells are ringing, survey the great world as it spins daily round under the eye of God. The sea which girdles the solid land is not so wide, nor deep, as the sea of unconverted life, which swelters and surges upon the habitations of human society. Three-fourths of earth's inhabitants are at this moment idolaters. Over this indubitable majority of our race, dominate the stern and terrible conditions of heathen life. Let only this one fact clear a space for itself in your thoughts. Of the ten hundred millions of breathing, living, thinking, human beings, our brothers and sisters in the flesh, our customers and employers in the market, more than seven hundred millions do not bow the knee to Jesus! What oppression of man by man is included in this portentous fact! What opposition to the gospel! What resistance to the divine purposes for humanity! What persecutions of converts at those far scattered spots where the Christian missionary has penetrated! What foulness and cruelty over all the surface in the domestic life! What barbarity and injustice in the life of the state! What wickedness, of which the poor soul is itself unconscious, in individuals! And yet the victims and agents of this idol-worship are on the same world with us. They are heirs with ourselves of all the wealth and skill which the earth contains. Their hands are reaching out for all the instruments of material power which have been sent to ourselves. And we and they are in the same home, under the same sky, looking up at the same sun and stars, the same waxing and waning moon; and they and we are to contend together for the empire of the world.

Can the contents of a future, which is charged with such a conflict, be the subject of indifference to any Christian heart? Yet we interrogate it in vain. We know indeed, that there can be but one issue in the long run to the struggle between good and evil. We know that ultimately all evil shall be abased, and every form and manifestation of sin receive its just recompense of reward. 'The day cometh—the great day—of the vengeance of the Lord.' But the time and the manner of its appearing we are not permitted to know. In vain we ask, whether free communities and godly worship are to continue, for long centuries yet, by the side of despotisms and huge idolatries? Are our children's children to be impeded as we have been in advancing the banner of the Lord? For ages still to come, is human life to be trodden down beneath the hoofs of evil? Abroad, are oppressions, and wars, and revolutions; at home, are crimes, and frauds, and hopeless suffering, to go on for ever? Shall the poor rot in unwholesome dwellings, and the ignorant remain ignorant as before? Is there to be no cessation, no amelioration, in our day, of the misery which social crime inflicts? And are new evils to spring up as fast as the old ones are destroyed? Or is the day of vengeance at hand? Are the axes even now sharpening which are to shiver the thrones of iniquity, and the temples of unclean superstition? And shall it be the unspeakable privilege of Christian men now living to see 'the last conflict of great principles' brought to a close, and the mild beneficent light of the cross spreading and taking captive all the nations of the earth?

But we ask in vain. There is only the rebound of the question on our own heart: The times and the seasons no man can know. Dates, and methods, and instruments of retribution, are known only to God. For us, too, the seals are on the book. 'And no man in heaven, nor in earth, neither under the earth,' is able to unloose them.[1] We can only be thankful—and we ought to be very thankful—that the book is in the hands of Christ, and that *He* has prevailed to unloose its seals.

[1] Prov. v. 22.

V.

DISCLOSURES.

'Be sure your sin will find you out.'
'There is nothing covered that shall not be revealed.'
'And I beheld when He had opened the sixth seal, ... and the kings of the earth, and the great men, and the rich men, and the chief captains, and the mighty men, and every bond man, and every free man, hid themselves in the dens, and in the rocks of the mountains; and said to the mountains and rocks, Fall on us, and hide us from the face of Him that sitteth on the throne, and from the wrath of the Lamb.'

IT has been asked, Is the unsealing of the book the issuing, or merely the revealing, of the judgments inscribed on its page? Very obviously it is both, sometimes the one, sometimes the other, oftentimes both together. The unsealing implies revelation; but it may be revelation of actual and present wrath against sin, or instruction in retribution, past or future. Preluding the great day of wrath and revelation of the righteous judgment of God, glimpses and foretastes of judgment are sent to man; but these glimpses may be sent through knowledge of the past, foreknowledge of the future, or experience of the present. In these various ways, Christ admits His people into the secrets of His providence. He involves them in passing retributions. He teaches them righteousness while His judgments are in the earth. The shadow which has followed the exile from the gates of Eden, descends on the path of His disciples. 'Wrath is revealed from heaven against all unrighteousness of men,' and His people are made to tremble under it.

Although concealed from human observation, and marching through seas of apparently accidental tumult and revolution, the acts of the divine government follow an orderly and natural development. They move in cycles, of which the cycles of seals and trumpets and vials, in the visions of John, are the symbols, and the cycles of sin on earth, the occasions and counterparts. Thus far those students of prophecy, who give their strength to the study of events, have a show of justification. Above the awful cycles of the word, Christ is imposing—the fulfilment above the prophecy—the not less awful cycles of human history. On earth, there is the beginning and consummation of sin; in the Bible, there is the beginning and consummation of prophetic statement in relation to the sin; from heaven, there is the beginning and consummation of the wrath which the sin calls forth. Just as, in the chapter which describes the opening of the seals, we have a progression of unsealings, and overlying these a progression of judgments; so, in the actual story of our race, and of every nation and individual of our race, there goes forward, in relation to every development of evil, what would answer to the first unsealing and its conquering rider, what would answer to the second and third, and so onward, till the consummation in the cries and anguish at the opening of the sixth. For if wickedness, in all its developments, has a growth, retribution has an equal growth. The one is sown, springs up, comes to a height, broadens and sheds its fruit. But corresponding to all that, the judgment of the Lord upon it develops, following the wicked growth step by step, rising, broadening, waxing stronger and more terrible, until at last it flashes out on the iniquity, and hews it down to the roots, and the evil-doer has to cry to the rocks and mountains to hide him from 'the wrath of the Lamb.'

Now in all such retributions, since they are prelusive, we may expect to find, not merely prelusions of the great final judgment itself, but also hints and testimonies more or less explicit of the principles on which that judgment shall be conducted. Of these principles, familiar to us through many a statement of Scripture, I shall now select three, that I may illustrate their presence in the judicial acts of Providence. The first is the well-known principle of appealing the justice of the doom to the consciousness of the sinner himself; the second is the manifestation to all the world of what was only known to that consciousness; the third is the use of the sin in bringing the hidden deed to light. There are other principles which will have play and influence in the great judgment at the close; but the illustration of the three I have named, may suffice to vindicate the conclusion,—to which the whole of what I have had to say about the sealed book points,—that the future judgment is simply a larger and fuller exhibition of the principles which are at work at present, by our side, in the ordinary judgments of Providence.

God begins by laying bare the sin to the sinner himself. The sinner may not know himself to be a sinner.

Disclosures.

He may be practising deception on himself. The 'iron pen' inscribes his guilt in his own consciousness. There is an impressive illustration of this principle of judgment in the history of David. There was evidently a time during which his shameful and cruel sin did not appear to be sin to him. Nearly a year seems to have gone past, before he was brought to a sense of his guilt. In the thirty-second Psalm he tells us the history of his life during that year. His sin was covered.[1] It did not shape itself to his thoughts as sin. It was something less, something else. Uriah fell in the battle, fell by the chances of war. Uriah's wife was David's subject, his vassal, his property, in a sense. And then, there was the licence of a king. Other kings had done such things: why not David? By whatever warp of falsehood, he did not see the sin to be sin.

The evil was committed partly in a palace, partly amid the confused noise of a battle-field. No eye but God's has seen the twofold wickedness in all its bad unfoldings. Uriah's body is buried—has had a soldier's burial. The instrument was a foeman's spear. The actual murderer did not imbrue his hands in his victim's blood. The channels to the discovery of the murder are all stopped up. The victim was a soldier, a man exposed to death. Such things were taking place every day. In this assurance, hiding his sin from himself, the murderer takes Uriah's wife to the palace. He resumes his accustomed duties, mingles with his counsellors, dispenses justice in the gate. But his peace is gone. His acknowledgment long afterwards is, that God's 'hand

[1] 'He that covereth his sin shall not prosper.'—Prov. xxviii. 13.

was heavy upon him, that his moisture was turned into the drought of summer.' What a history is revealed in these two lines! It is the history of unconfessed sin in all ages. The memory of his sin is within him now as a ball of burning brass. He cannot forget it; cannot put away the thought of it; cannot think calmly about it. ' My moisture is turned into the drought of summer.' Ah! we all know something of what that means. The sin and its attendant circumstances are coming up before his conscience more vividly every hour. It haunts him like a spirit from the dead. It confronts him, king though he is, in every crowd. He meets it in the gate, he sees it in the palace; it visits him in his dreams; it has murdered sleep. It prevents his prayers; talks to him in his solitude; pursues him into the council chamber; puts a blight upon his life, his home, his health. Day and night, night and day, God's 'hand is heavy' upon him. With a fierce, unresting perseverance, it clings to him. Among his soldiers, he sees but one form—the form of his victim. Among the sweetest and most solemn sounds, he hears but one cry—the death-cry of his victim. The earth is turned for him into one continuous battle-field, on which the foul deed is daily repeated. '*That* is Uriah, the noble-hearted Uriah. *That* is the foeman's weapon. But *this, this* is the hand that wielded it.' The hand is David's own. The conviction becomes clearer every day, burns through the wrappings of self-deception, puts aside battle, foeman, royal licence, sovereign right—comes straight at his own heart. Nathan only utters what is already written by God's pen on his own conscience. 'Thou art the man.'

shines out upon him from within. His refuge of lies is swept away. His pride is broken. He is down in the dust before the all-seeing eye. 'I acknowledge my sin: mine iniquity I have not hid.'

Blessed is the man who, seeing the sinfulness of his sin, and the impossibility of covering it himself, flees to God, as David did, for concealment of it. In mercy God displays it to the conscience. In mercy God has provided the means by which the foul conscience is cleansed. If the sinner repair to that mercy, his transgression is covered by the very God he has offended. But if the cleansing which is in that mercy is neglected,—if there is no opening of the soul to the admonitions of God, no turning back by confession and repentance to the divine bosom,—conscience, heart, and life take on a deeper and darker imprint of the sin, and the sinner is hurried on to a public and terrible exposure of his iniquity.

This is a hard truth for evil-doers. They do not care to think of the exposures which the Lord is keeping in reserve for them. They do not care to think at all of the future for which they are heaping up treasures of wrath. Their practical conviction is, that they are living in the world of a blind ruler. 'The Lord hideth His face: He will never see.' They will not believe, that the whole domain of evil, past and present, lies open to His eye. They cannot hide the evil they have done, where that eye will not search it out. They cannot bury the past record of their lives, where that eye will not survey its contents. From beginning to end their evil deeds have been visible to the Lord. He saw them in their germ:

He saw them in their full growth. If He forbore to strike, that only proved His compassion. 'He is long-suffering, not willing that any should perish.' He gives space to the sinner for repentance. But all the while, His pure Spirit beholds, and resents, the hidden and unrequited sin. And in whatever depth of heart or life, the evil-doer may try to conceal his wickedness, and by whatever tangle of plan or pretence, he may seek to disguise it, his attempt will be vain. The thought of the plotting Pharisees, the design of the traitor Judas,—the cunningest, most hidden disloyalty to His name or cause, in any heart,—He knows it all. There is no crack or crevice, no wilderness or ocean depth, where evil can be hidden from His view. That eye follows it, searches it, confronts it evermore. From the awful light of that presence it cannot escape. The universe is His, and refuses to conceal it. If it made its bed in hell, it would be confronted there. 'There is no darkness nor shadow of death where the workers of iniquity may hide themselves.' There are no rocks that will fall upon them, and hide them from His wrath. They, with all the evil they have done, lie open before the eye of Him, 'Who will bring to light the hidden things of darkness.'

I believe this to have been the principal lesson intended by the doom on Ananias and Sapphira. It was necessary to assert this truth at the time. A new era was coming to the birth. God was vouchsafing a fuller revelation of himself. The circumstances of the early Church required its members to sweep the whole circle of truth. They were receivers for the ages to come. It was their function to realize, and express, the facts and feelings of all Christian faith and life. Their consciousness was made to glow with truths which come slowly, and one by one, in ordinary times. Descents of the Spirit, tongues, healings, apostleships, miraculous guidance, entered into their experience, and brought the eternal world habitually near. They had been receiving revelations of the Lord, as the Lord of mercy and healing. Daily, they were made to see and realize Him as the Lord of truth and power. They must now behold Him as the Lord of holiness and wrath. The awful truth must enter powerfully into their souls, that He is Judge as well as Saviour, and that, as Judge, He stands at all the doors of life; that He is against evil in all the earth; that He will not tolerate it in the Church; and that, out of the lowest deep, He will bring it up into the light, and reprove and punish it. It was the miserable lot of Ananias and Sapphira to evoke the revelation of this truth.

The circumstances were peculiar. A great fervour of love had descended on the Church. Its members felt that they were not their own; that all they possessed belonged to the Master and His work. Many of them sold their possessions, and transferred the price to the treasury of the Church. It was a noble sacrifice. It would not be in human nature to witness it unmoved. A glow of admiration from the flock, a glow of approval from the Shepherd, were certain to go forth upon the noble givers.

'Could we not share this honour? Could we not have the glory, the distinction, the moral influence, of those who have given all, *without* giving all?' This was the question, which that misguided couple put to each other.

There was no necessity upon them to take such a step. It was no law of the Church. No obligation lay on any member to imitate the sacrifices of those who had sold their all. It was entirely voluntary. But Ananias and his wife would have the honour. They looked at the possibility of working out their plan. They saw how it could be done. They would sell their possessions; they would keep back part of the price; they would give what remained as the whole. They 'agreed together' in this wickedness. They did it all in secret. No doubt, they would bind each other to secrecy. No ear of man was to receive the tale of their deception. No eye of man could search their proceedings, and find out the wickedness. Darkness brooded over their sin. In ordinary times they might have carried out their wickedness without discovery. It might not occur to them that theirs was an exceptional time. The probability was, that they would not be discovered, that they would not even be suspected. They would deliberate on all that. They saw, or thought they saw, that the thing was safely buried out of sight. At all events, they came up into the presence of the Church, with their spoken and embodied lie. Ananias came first, but we may look at the two together. They came to do an act which should appear a liberal one, a self-sacrificing one, in the eyes of God's people. They brought the portion which they had resolved to give, and they laid it at the apostles' feet, and they laid it there as the unbroken price. You can fancy the hum of admiration going round the circle, or more likely, the whisper of thankful prayer over this new proof of the Spirit's power. The lie, to all human insight, is completely hidden. It is hidden by the words with which the gift is given. It is hidden by the precaution which the two had previously taken. It is hidden by the Christian bearing they had put on, and by the whole tone and manner of their appearance. It is hidden in the depths of their guilty hearts. And yet it was not hidden. It never had been hidden. The Lord had seen it from its first beginning. The Lord had followed it from the hour when it was a suggestion of Satan, until it was embodied in the hollow show of a Christian sacrifice and spiritual grace. The Church was deceived: He is not deceived. The Church was mocked: He is not mocked. He cleaves the darkness by an awful flash of inspiration. He lays open to His servant Peter the whole transaction in all its black deceitfulness. Ananias and Sapphira had done a great wrong;—they had lied, not unto men, but unto God. There was no concealment more for their lie. The Lord dragged it into shameful publicity. In the sight of those very eyes, to gain whose smile they had planned their evil deed, He erected His judgment-seat; and there and then, He slew them in His wrath.

Evil cannot hide itself out of Christ's sight. Sooner or later, the hurtful thing is exposed. Sooner or later, the souls who have made themselves one with it are dragged into the light. There may be long concealment, long miles to traverse before the exposure; but at length, in time, or beyond time, the point is reached. The evil-doers, on their way through life, may occupy positions which shall act as screens to them; the events of their lives may be associated with other events, which may seem to put a wall between their guilt and its discovery; but it is only a lengthening out of the journey. The inevitable hour arrives at last. Sin and exposure are inextricably joined. The darkness is cleft, and the books are opened, and the tale which sin has written is laid completely bare.

In the case I have narrated, the circumstances were urgent and peculiar. The exposure was taken out of the ordinary course, and made miraculous. But it was only the *manner*, not the fact, that was miraculous. Left to themselves, and to the influences upon themselves of their sin, Ananias and Sapphira would probably have developed into a shape, which itself would have become an exposure of their wickedness. In one way or other, and without any miracle, what they had done was certain at length to be laid bare. But this remark brings me to the third principle I named—the principle of using the sin to find the sinner out. The popular conviction is, that crime, especially aggravated crime, is certain to be found out. 'Murder will out;' and 'one day or other, one way or other, guilt will be tracked to its lair.' The judicial exposure and human punishment are understood to be the 'finding out.' But this is only a part of the truth, and, within these limits, not always a certain part. There is a discovery of guilt which underlies all the investigations of society. Apart from every judicial process here, even if there should be no judicial process, and if the guilt should never be found out on earth, a most real detection has already taken place. The crime itself, in the moral history of the criminal, is detection. This, whatever its form may be, is the black entry of guilt, the divinely written doom-word, on the life of the evil-doer,

'Be sure your sin shall find you out.' Your *sin!* Not any appliances of earthly justice, nor circumstances, nor accidents, but the sin itself.

Step into this criminal court. A noted poisoner is in the dock. He is accused of poisoning his friend, and antecedently his own wife. You listen to the testimony. You listen to arguments on the evidence. You see the evolution of exposure—exposure of the criminal and his crime. So far as the legal process goes, the exposure is searching and complete. The crime is thoroughly, unmistakeably traced home, and traced home to him. The unhappy man had taken extraordinary caution in the administration of the poison. He had given it in brandy and water, given it in broth, given it in medicine. He gave it as a medical man, gave it in co-operation with other medical men. He was present when his victim was ill, was present when he died. He assisted to coffin him, to examine his body after death. The poison by which life was destroyed was not found in the dead body. Detection seemed impossible. Yet detection was reached. All his precautions were vain. Threads of incidental observations mesh around the murderer, and enclose him as in a net. Servant-girls, cab-drivers, shop-boys, postmasters, doctors, sick-nurses, attorneys, usurers, horseracers,—people intent, at the time the murder was being committed, on their own concerns, not suspecting murder,—remember things, looks, words, actions of the accused, which, taken together, declare him to be the murderer. The murderer is found out. But all this comes far short of the process which Christ superintends. This is not the man's *sin* finding him out.

Perhaps there never was a criminal trial in which medical testimony bore a more conspicuous part than it did in the trial I am referring to. Strychnine was the poison which caused the death; but science had no chemical tests at the time by which this particular poison could be detected after death. Yet, wonderful to say, without such tests, the medical testimony was completely and conclusively given. The symptoms accompanying the death were identified with those which that poison, and only that poison, would originate. Not only so. By a diabolical skill in the application of poison, the murderer had used a less virulent drug, to prepare his victims for the more effectual action of the strychnine. This preparatory poison was found in the dead bodies, in the body of the poor wife especially, with remarkable precision of detail. Science told the day, and the very hour of the day, when the doses were administered. It revealed the number, the strength, and the succession of the doses. 'This was given so many hours before she died; this other, so many hours before that.' Yet even this, wonderful though it was, comes short of the process which Christ superintends. This is still not the man's *sin* finding him out.

No; to witness this process, to see the instrument which found him out, you must go far back in the history of the man. You must go back to a date when his hands were still free from blood. The murder was not the sin. The sin was the selling himself to do evil, years before the murder was done. It was the yielding up of all that energy, all that intellect, all that love which his crimes and his pleasures exacted, to crimes and pleasures instead of God. That was the man's sin. That was the sin which found him out. I can easily believe, he did not intend to be a murderer, when he began his career. Murder was the unexpected development, the unforeseen consequence and natural fruit, of his sin. When the sin was ripe, he did the murder. But he did it as the bound thrall of his sin. The murder itself was the finding out. Even as his victims were prepared for the swifter action of the strychnine by antimony, so he, by his previous choice of principles, and by his bad career, for its black and murderous close. He had lived a wild life in connection with horse-racing—a life of mad excitement and base pleasure-seeking. And the elements of that life—the gambling, the betting, the losses by betting, the borrowing to repair these losses, the forgery to replace what he had borrowed—were the preparations by which his own soul was drugged. Murder was the outcome, the revelation by blood, of him and his wicked life.

Ah! if we could unfold the secrets of that invisible world which Christ, as Judge, rules over, and which surrounds us all,—if we could lay bare the actual, inner stages of a guilty man's career,—we would then see how, not science, nor circumstantial evidence, nor ocular testimony, but only sin, can find him out. Not as attempting to unfold those secrets, but simply as suggesting the natural history of sin in a wicked life, I invite you to go back in the history of this criminal, to the first step in his bad career—to his first decisive choice of a gambler's life. The Bible speaks of the kingdom and 'power of darkness.' I believe the race-course, which was the scene of this man's gambling, to be one of the most active manifestations of this kingdom. I believe the excitement, the hazard, the speculation, the betting, the gains, the losses, the borrowings, the lendings, to be so many instrumentalities of this 'power of darkness.' Out of that betting arises the necessity for money; out of that necessity, the borrowing at sixty per cent.; out of that borrowing, the forgery; out of that forgery, the dismal thought of murder. Note the inevitable steps. Borrowing at sixty per cent. to meet the debts of gambling; forgery to escape these debts; at last, murder to retrieve the forgery. The man is no longer himself. He is the thrall of the power of evil, to which, years before, he sold himself. Whether out of the man, or in the man, I do not say; but the thought arises, the black, foul thought of murder. It hovers over the sin-driven crowds of the racing circle he frequents, seeking an instrument. It comes to him, finds an open door, enters, takes possession, and drives him down its steeps into the abysses of death. It says virtually to the man: 'Be my slave to do this—*this!*' And the man, his conscience seared, his will broken, wasted, weak by previous sin—the man yields. He does the deed. And, doing it, his sin has found him out.

It is therefore the sin itself which is the terrible, the inevitable detector. It is this, which inscribes upon the being of the sinner the unconcealable brand. Though circumstances, consequences, witnesses, experiments, tests, detectives, judges, juries, all should fail, this is certain to succeed. It follows the sinner from the hour he admits it into his being, through every subsequent movement of his life. It drives him on, and down, and down for ever. He cannot escape from it; it cannot be separated from his life. It comes closer to him every day, entangles him more completely every hour, puts its foul hand upon him, throws him into its pits, stamps its hoof-mark on his brow, and brands him all over with its ineradicable and unmistakeable verdict. That is its sad commission received from the Lord. The Lord did not make it, did not bid it into this world; but now that it is here, by the wrong choice of man, this is its work—to find out the sinner, to spot him all over with the spots of iniquity, to bring him into the presence of the light from which he has been fleeing, and in that light to reveal him, all marked and written over with the awful signatures of sin.

The evil-doer *becomes the evil* which he does. Just as children of the light are changed by the light into actual light, so the children of darkness become the very darkness they love. It may be said, that two things advance on parallel lines towards the judgment-seat: the claim of God upon the moral being of man, and the moral being itself. The claim upon us is, to become vessels of light, of truth, of life. If we meet that claim, our being heightens daily in capacity and worth. If we refuse to meet it, if we shut out God's light, our being becomes blind, and feeble, and stunted—a mere record of transgression and sin. But it becomes this, by the side of the undying claim. And the two together—the divine claim, and the soul which has refused that claim—shall come face to face, at the judgment-bar. And there, in the very presence of the light which has been despised, the stunted, dwarfed, blinded, sin-stained, moral being must stand, instead of that perfection which ought to have been.

Part Second.

THE OPEN BOOK;

OR,

BOOK OF THE JUDGING WORD.

'And I took the little book out of the angel's hand, and ate it up; and it was in my mouth sweet as honey; and as soon as I had eaten it, my belly was bitter. And he said unto me, Thou must prophesy again before many peoples, and nations, and tongues, and kings.'

John.

'Thy words were found, and I did eat them; and Thy word was unto me the joy and rejoicing of mine heart. . . . Why is my pain perpetual, and my wound incurable, which refuseth to be healed?'

Jeremiah.

'Son of man, eat that thou findest: eat this roll, and go speak unto the house of Israel. So I opened my mouth, and He caused me to eat that roll. . . . And it was in my mouth as honey for sweetness. And He said unto me, Son of man, go, get thee unto the house of Israel, and speak with my words unto them. . . . But the house of Israel will not hearken unto thee.'

Ezekiel.

'For judgment I am come into this world, that they which see not might see, and they which see might be made blind.'

The Lord.

'If our gospel be hid, it is hid to them that are lost. In whom the god of this world hath blinded the minds of them which believe not, lest the light of the glorious gospel of Christ, who is the image of God, should shine unto them.'

Paul.

I.

THE LIGHT OF THE WORLD.

'The victory of the early Church was not due wholly to intellectual remedies, such as the answers of apologists, but mainly to moral; to the inward perception generated of the adaptation of Christianity to supply the spiritual wants of human nature. As the heathen realized the sense of sin, they felt intuitively the suitability of salvation through Christ; as they witnessed the transforming power of belief in Him, they felt the inward testimony to the truth of Christianity. The external evidence of religion had its office in the early Church; . . . but the internal evidences—Christ, Christianity, Christendom—were the most potent proofs offered; the doctrine of an atoning Messiah filling the heart's deepest longings, and the lives of Christians embodying heavenly virtues.'—FARRAR: *History of Free Thought*.

ROM the beginning of the eighth chapter of the Apocalypse to the close of the eleventh, we find a distinct cycle of visions. The seven angels who stand before God, receive their trumpets at the commencement of the events recorded in these chapters. At the close, the last of the seven angels has sounded, and the series of events has come to an end. It is in the heart of these events that the second judgment-book is displayed.

An almost entire contrast of features distinguishes this second book from the first. The first was in heaven in the hands of Christ: this is sent down to earth by the hands of an angel. The one was to a great extent inscrutable, written within and without, and sealed by seven seals: the other is little, open, intended to be read and known. The one was an object of ecstatic contemplation to the inhabitants of heaven: this, in some real way, is food for those of earth. The purpose of the display of the one was the comfort of the suffering Church: the purpose of the mission of the other is the conversion of kings and nations. If these contrasts be looked at together, the inference is irresistible, that as, in the sealed book, we have a symbol of the providence of Him whose path is in the deep, in this 'little book open,' we have the symbol of that gospel, which has been revealed from heaven, which we are to receive as our life and food, and to preach to every creature in the world.

It is a *book*, for it contains the thoughts and utterances of God. It is an *open* book, for it is a revelation of these thoughts to us. And it is a *little* book, for it contains principles mainly; and in comparison with the results it aims at, and also in the judgment of men, is a small unlikely thing—a mere germ—no bigger than a mustard seed: a very little thing—a word—but a word carrying in its heart the salvation of the world.

In the deepest sense, no doubt, Christ himself is the reality symbolized in this book. 'I am the light of the world.' He is God's revelation of himself to man, God's provision for the spiritual wants of our race. But, on the other hand, Christ and the truth concerning Christ are one. What we call 'the gospel' is just Christ, the Word, expressed in human speech, and delivered to us as good news concerning the Father and himself. Our Lord admits us into the innermost secret and vital character of the book when He says, 'I came forth from the Father: I speak the things which I have seen with the Father: I came forth to do the will of the Father.' What Christ has seen with the Father, therefore, what Christ has revealed of the Father, what Christ came forth to do for the Father: these are the first and main facts, the primary rays of the light, which shine upon us from the open book.

But we would have a very inadequate, at all events a vague, idea of the reality symbolized by this second book, if only this much were understood. The open book is the gospel, but it is that gospel translated into life and character. It is still the word, but it is the word 'made flesh:' very really a book of God, intended by God to be 'known and read of all men;' but a book 'written not with ink, but with the Spirit of the living God; not in tables of stone, but in fleshly tables of the heart.'[1] The oneness between Christ and His people, and between His life and theirs, results in the fact that they, in a most real way, are to the world all that He is,—a divine life manifested to men, a light shining in a dark place. And therefore He says, without any qualification, 'YE are the light of the world.' Now this very fact is pressed on our notice in the details of the vision in which the open book is displayed. John, who in the previous vision was the representative of the suffering Church, is in this one the representative of the Church's teaching. He receives the open book, that by means of it he may go forth and 'prophesy.' But it will be observed that his selection to this work is determined by the previous influence upon

[1] 2 Cor. iii. 2, 3.

him of the book itself. He is first commanded to eat the book, and only after that commissioned to carry its message to the kings and nations to whom it was to be addressed. In other words, the prophet who is to declare its contents, must believe them and become them first. The truths by which he is to renew the life of the world, must previously be the nourishment of his own. He must himself become the open book. Thus, a second time, we are in the presence of the fact—a fact which reproduces itself wherever we find a book of judgment mentioned in the Bible—that these book symbols point not to formal material manuscripts, but to realities of life, and faith, and practice in the spirit and conduct of human beings. In the sealed book, man expresses the wrath; in the open book, the love, of God. Although the latter symbol, looked at apart from its surroundings, would fitly express and find its deepest significance in the personal Christ as the light of the world, it is abundantly obvious that it is Christ translated into human life which is symbolized in the vision in which John represented the preaching of the word.

The life and doctrines of Christ pass, by regeneration and faith, into the life and speech of the men who are to proclaim them, and they become to their generation what Christ himself would be in their place. The great cause advances by the advance among men of 'the word made flesh.' Evermore, that word is passing into flesh. The 'open secret' is drawn into the life of prophet and disciple, and becomes a life within their life, and their very life; and *by this life* thereafter—this life as the manifestation of the divine life—the world is to be conquered.

'YE,' as truly as the doctrines are, 'YE'—the living men and women who believe the doctrines, and are the incarnation of the doctrines, and, in consequence, the Church of Christ,—'YE are the light of the world,' that open book whose message is to be announced to 'peoples, and nations, and tongues, and kings.'

The sphere of the operation of this second book is 'the world'—the world in its sin-trodden, idol-worshipping, and God-renouncing aspects. The men who compose it are men who '*worship devils, and idols of gold, and silver, and brass, and stone, and wood.*' And the ultimate result of the promulgation of the book is this, that '*the kingdoms of the world are become the kingdoms of our Lord and of His Christ.*' For my particular purpose it is not necessary to specialize the sphere by time or place. It is the 'world.' It may be that manifestation of it which we find in heathen lands, or in the mammon-worship of civilised Christendom, or any past or future manifestation of heathen principles in social life. No one development of worldliness can exhaust the application of the vision. Wherever the worldly element exists, and rises up to oppose the progress of the gospel, this vision of the open book repeats its lessons to the Church.

It is a notable circumstance, in preparing our minds to see the judicial character of this book, that its revelation is represented as coinciding with a crisis in the development of the world on which it acts. It comes, as the Lord did, in the fulness of time. It comes after other measures have been tried in vain. It comes as the last and strongest appeal of God. His merciful severity towards the sins of heathenism had produced no fruit.

There was no repentance of the evil life. The time of probation was therefore drawing to a close. The angel of the book, setting his one foot on the sea, and his other on the land,—covering in this way the whole sphere which heathenism had darkened,—swears by the living Maker of sea and land, that the hour of its downfall has struck. Its 'time shall be no more.' No more time, no further space, shall be granted to it. Its time of evil-doing, of hostility to God's cause, is at an end. It has lasted long enough to demonstrate its utter unworthiness to possess or influence any sphere of human life. Corruption and self-destruction have been the fruits of the principles at its heart. The hour has come when the divine purposes imperatively demand repentance or destruction. Coincident with this hour is, what may be named the hour of the open book,—the critical moment when it strikes in to fulfil, by conversion or condemnation, its appointed task in the completion of the mystery of God upon the earth.

And it is just here, on the very threshold of the task to which he is called, that the experience of the prophet is made use of, to foreshadow the sad character of the path which his message and himself have to tread. He is sent forth on his mission with a burden of pain on his soul. The book which was sweet in his mouth becomes bitter in his belly. Some great sorrow darkens over the joy which the first taste of the heavenly food imparts. What is the secret of this sorrow? What underlies this transition from sweetness to bitterness? It cannot be an accidental touch of description. Some real harmony binds together the sorrowful heart and the conflict on which it enters. Some tragic element somewhere is ready to spring to light. To discover what this is, we must glance for a moment at the chapter in which the conflict is traced.

It is the eleventh chapter which contains this history. In this chapter are traced, from the first entrance of the truth to its ultimate issues on those to whom it is sent, the results of gospel preaching. The symbols change with the changing developments of the conflict. The prophet who has been fed by the book becomes the measurer of the temple, and the temple itself: those who have not yet tasted his food are 'the court which is without the temple.' The temple changes into 'the two witnesses, the two olive-trees, the two candlesticks standing before the God of the earth;' the outer court, on the other hand, becomes the persecutor of the witnesses— 'the beast that ascendeth out of the bottomless pit, the great city, the Sodom and Egypt,' which crucified our Lord; but under all this change and progression of symbol, advances the history of the conflict of Christianity with an idol-worshipping and godless world.

It will be observed, that twofold results flow from the preaching of the prophet of the book. A temple rises, and also a court outside of the temple. Witnesses lift up their testimony, and persecutors their sword. The river of life is as clearly visible as the wilderness it seeks to reclaim. But in the end, the shadows rest on the unreclaimed waste; the gloomier aspects of the conflict have possession of our mind. You see the temple marking out by its simple presence a sphere of life which is *not* temple; you see the sphere which is *not* temple—the outer-court-life, darkening into malice and hell-born persecution of Christ,—becoming Sodom, Egypt, and the beast. Although the witnesses themselves have a glorious resurrection and reward, yet woe chases woe athwart the field of conflict still; Christ comes forth in anger to destroy them which destroy the earth; and the scene closes amid 'lightnings, and voices, and thunderings, and an earthquake, and great hail.'

It seems to me that we are intended to see beneath these tempestuous symbols, the tragic side of gospel preaching—the sad story of its becoming a savour of death unto death to all who reject it. The bitterness which the prophet feels is the inevitable sorrow of one who sees a doom descending on the souls he would save. The spectacle of an unconverted, persecuting world, breaks upon his view, and his soul is filled with anguish. Rivers of waters run down his eyes. The joy of his own salvation only deepens the sadness with which he contemplates the calamity of those who refuse to be saved. In the light of the Father's love, resting on his own life, he has a perpetual joy. In the view of the fire which is to consume his Father's enemies, he becomes, like his Master, a man of sorrows.

Alas! this is no strange or exceptional element in the experience of those who are called either to preach or extend the gospel. It is the experience of every witness for the truth who ever lived. I find it in the old prophets, when they longed for a lodging-place in the wilderness, where they might weep day and night for the sins of the people. I find it in the sorrow of the Lord of life. I find it in all His apostles. The recorded experiences of missionaries and ministers of the word bear witness to it. It is a constant experience with preachers of the gospel. Each of them has to shed his tears over unsaved Jerusalem. Each of them must pass on to the sharp conviction, that the word which saves is a sword as well. On those who reject it, the gospel issues a deeper condemnation. The open book—the book which tells of a Saviour's love—becomes a book of judgment to the world.

This, then, is the fact I am to illustrate now,—that the gospel is a book of doom. But I could have no satisfaction in dealing with such a fact, unless I were first to testify, that a result so sad is contrary to the primal purpose of the gospel. Retribution is the 'strange work' of the gospel. 'God sent not His Son into the world to condemn the world, but that the world through Him might be saved.' He has no 'pleasure' in the death of the wicked. The yearning of His heart is, that sinners would turn to Him and live. And, therefore, putting thoughts of retribution and judgment aside for a moment, it will be good to recruit our minds by a glance at that gospel, whose open page reveals the story of God's love to man.

The gospel is God's remedy for a fallen world. Instead of smiting the evil-doer with immediate wrath, He comes forth to save him. The gospel is the declaration of the righteous God, that judgment shall not at once be executed on the human race. It is the assurance, that a space for repentance has been cleared out by the blood of Christ. It is God's loving message to the children who have wandered from the home of their Father. It is God's welcome to sin-torn and weary spirits. At the inmost core of it, is the purpose to save. It stretches out loving arms towards all the ends of the earth, to gather the lost ones back to the fold.

Everything the sinner needs for his salvation is in the gospel. No shadow rests on this salvation. It will allow no questioning of the Saviour's willingness or power to save. It is the clear, unambiguous offer of immediate and abiding mercy to every sinner of mankind. Our spirits are borne by it into the abyss of the Father's heart. We see Him replying to the sin of the world by the gift of His Son. We see the Son going up the steeps of Calvary for our salvation. We see Him dying to subdue mankind by His love. We see the loving One laying His bleeding hands on the heart of enmity. We see Him folding the rebel to His breast. The mystery of the ages and the universe is laid bare to us. He comes to tell us of our Father. He descends into our darkness, and the light of heaven is on the earth. He touches the rocky heart of our race, and streams of divine life burst forth. And out of His blessed lips, and from the well-springs of love in the heart of Jehovah, over the troubled waters of human wretchedness, to the unquiet, sin-darkened spirit of man, comes the still small voice of offered mercy: 'On Him have I laid the iniquity of you all.' 'Though your sins be as scarlet, they shall be white as snow.' 'Hear ye Him,' and in your souls, and over all the earth, 'the wilderness and the solitary place shall be glad.' 'He that believeth on Him, though he were dead, yet shall he live.'

On this subject, then, let there be no misunderstanding. The grand purpose of the gospel is salvation. Whether it reaches the sinner in the simple word, or by the personal agents, the *first* purpose of the message in the open book is to save. But beyond this lies the other and awful fact I am to illustrate, that to those who reject its offers, it is condemnation and death.

The regulative principle of Christ's government must be sought for in the cross. The cross lies at the heart of creation, and we must expect to discover it in all the judgments of Providence. The 'Lamb that was slain'[1] is on the throne of the universe, and all the movements of the universe must be sprinkled with His blood. A new element has been added to human life; and it is such an element as must alter entirely the relation of man to divine things. The world is not the same world with as without the cross. There is a way opened up out of all the sin and sorrow of earth; graciously opened up; opened freely and impartially; opened for every sinner of mankind, and opened by the blood of Christ. By that very circumstance, man is imperatively summoned into the presence of the cross, to make his decision for time and eternity. He cannot get away from it. It defers, but does not abolish, the day of reckoning. Christ died on that cross for the guilty: those who continue guilty will encounter the cross on the day of judgment. This will be their condemnation, that the cross had shed its light on their path. Everything in human life must now take on an aspect of Calvary. For good or for evil, Calvary shines forth as light and new

[1] Rev. xiii. 8.

responsibility on conscience, thought, work, relationship, and character. 'If I had not come and spoken unto them, they had not had sinned; but now they have no cloak for their sin.' As justly as He exacts obedience for the gifts bestowed in creation, He exacts obedience for the gifts bestowed in the cross. The cross supplies the light by which He will separate the righteous from the wicked, and the principles on which the judgments on the wicked shall go forth.

And thus it arises that the very best thing in the world of truth—the revelation of God to man—may and must become a book of doom to those who reject it. I might name the illustration of this fact, which is to follow, *the Natural History of the Gospel in its results on the world.* That is the history unfolded in the vision of the open book. And the results it sets before us are these: First, by mere contrast with the evil in the world, the gospel is condemnation. Next, by exciting the hatred and cruelty of those it reproves, it deepens that condemnation. Finally, by the altered circumstances which it creates, in which adhesion to Christ's cause or absolute rejection of it is imperative, it determines the irretrievable separation of the wicked to their doom.

II.

THE LIGHT REVEALING THE DARKNESS.

'This is the condemnation, that light has come into the world, and men loved darkness rather than light, because their deeds were evil.'

'But the court which is without the temple leave out, and measure it not.'

AN illustration of the history of the gospel becoming a book of doom, I start with the statement, that a mass of ungodly life may exist and act, without knowing that it is ungodly. The processes of individual experience repeat themselves in the wider spheres of social life. Before the law comes, sin is dead,—is ignorant that it is sin. The light that reveals it to itself, that enters into it, and gives it consciousness of its own character, has not yet been shed, and the wickedness festers on with as little feeling as a corpse.

Even we, with all our Christian knowledge, have, for example, but a faint idea of the awful abysses in the world of heathenism. We speak of heathen life without realizing what the name conceals. We say, 'China,' 'India,' 'Africa,' but do not take into consideration the elements which compose their social and religious condition. And when the actual vices are named to us, as in the first chapter of the Epistle to the Romans, where the veil is lifted by the hand of such a master as Paul, and the spectacle as it displays itself in the light of God, is laid open to our view, we shrink away from the description, as something exceptional and far away; yet that description in Romans is literally true. Abhorrent and disgusting as the vices are, of which we have there the catalogue, they are the familiar habits of heathen life in every age, and they are indulged in, without remorse or shame. Missionaries find the same practices, and the same unconsciousness of their iniquity, in the countries to which they repair at present. Wherever the gospel comes into conflict with a world, from which the true God has been excluded, it comes into the presence, at the very outset, of an unconscious mass of immorality and crime.

In this respect 'the world' is the same in all ages and in every land. Circumstances which alter its outer garb or name, do not affect this feature of its life. If there be no ideal of a purer life, its wicked practices are carried on with little knowledge of their wickedness. In the fashionable life of modern civilisation, in the foul and cruel idol-worship of Calabar, away back among the nations of the Roman Empire, the three great roots of worldliness, the lust of the flesh, the lust of the eye, and the pride of life, send up their supplies of moral death to a people, who fancy they are drawing into their veins the sap of a perfect existence.

Let us picture to ourselves, therefore, a society of which those lusts are the animating principles. Let us try to understand what it is, before the light of a better life falls on its putrescent elements. We shall then be in circumstances to understand how the gospel, from the very first, must be a judgment-book. Look first at the *sensuality in the cravings and delights of the world.* It is a mere animal. Gluttony, drunkenness, prostitution, adultery, are words which express, with a deceitful brevity, the kind of life it leads. Greedy satisfaction of the brutal appetites; cruel disregard of the well-being of others in the satisfaction of these appetites; passionate outbreaking of anger, malice, revenge, and jealousy, when these are thwarted;—these are the manifestations of its grovelling sensuality. Look next *at the vanity of its admirations and worship.* It is a fool in things spiritual. It walks by sight. It must have a beauty and a god which it can handle, and 'invest,' and turn materially to account. An invisible glory, an inner purity, rewards and ecstasies of the spirit, it cannot understand. 'Show us your God' is its hereditary taunt to the Christian. The god of the world must not delay his coming, must become 'cash down,' fine houses, splendid apparel, stylish entertainments, pictures, amusements, books, at once. In folly like this there is no room for faith, or any true loyalty or reverence. 'O Lord, how great are Thy works! and Thy thoughts are very deep. A brutish man knoweth not; neither doth a fool understand this.'[1]

It is only the natural consequence of this want of faith and reverence, that *in its social life this world is a tyrant.* The common apprehension is, that there was more tyranny in old times than now; and that, of ancient tyrannies, the tyranny of the Roman Empire was the worst. 'To see the old world in its worst estate, we turn to the age of the satirists and of Tacitus, when all the different streams

[1] Ps. xcii. 5, 6.

of evil coming from east, west, north, south,—the vices of barbarism and the vices of civilisation, remnants of ancient cults, and the latest refinements of luxury and impurity,—met and mingled on the banks of the Tiber."[1] But the historians and satirists who depict that old world, almost seem to be portraying the world which is around ourselves.[2] We see the same two classes, the privileged and the servile, dependent, yet standing apart, and mutually repelling each other. We see the same old contrast of boundless luxury and harrowing distress. Over all the English and European world, of which we form a part, magnificent residences meet us in one street, and in another, hovels and dens where it is death to live. On the very field where toiling multitudes can hardly earn

---

[1] Jowett, vol. ii. 75.

[2] 'These great works (architectural, etc., of Rome) may be safely taken as emblems of the magnitude, strength, grandeur, and solidity of the empire; but they are emblems no less of the tyranny and cruelty which had presided over its formation, and of the general suffering which pervaded it. The statues with which the metropolis and the Roman houses were profusely decorated, had been brought from plundered provinces, and many of them had swelled the triumphs of conquerors on the Capitol. The amphitheatres were built for shows of gladiators, and were the scenes of a bloody cruelty, which had been quite unknown in the licentious exhibition of the Greek theatre. The roads, baths, harbours, aqueducts, had been constructed by slave labour; and the country villas which the Italian traveller lingered to admire, were themselves vast establishments of slaves.'—*Conybeare and Howson's St Paul*, vol. i. ch. 1.

'As regards the manners and mode of life of the Romans, their great object at this time was the acquisition and possession of money. Their moral conduct, which had been corrupt enough before the social war, became still more so by their systematic plunder and rapine. Immense riches were accumulated and squandered upon brutal pleasures.'—*Ibid.*, quotation from *Niebuhr's Lectures*.

a sustenance, riches are accumulated without principle, and squandered in frivolous joys. The lines and colours of the old pictures are those of modern life. In every age, the spirit of the world is despotic and cruel. It comes to be ministered to, not to minister. It must be surrounded with splendour, at whatever cost to others. It sacrifices a million lives to build a pyramid. It establishes negro slavery. It promotes war. It fills the earth with oppression. It tramples the toiling masses into crime, and, under the cloak of justice, its feet are swift to shed their blood. It has no ear for the cry of the afflicted; and it leaves the poor and the sick to perish in the street.

It is into this world of sin and evil-doing, this heartless, irreverent, and brutish life, so splendid in its outward aspects, so sad in its inner depths,—this world crammed and loaded with uncleanness, vanity, and oppression,—that the gospel has to advance. Along the edge and into the midst of precisely such a mass of black and seething wickedness, Paul and the first preachers, Luther and the first reformers, and Christian missionaries and ministers of every generation, have had to carry the banner of the cross. It advances its pure ideal of human life into the heart of societies, whose life-blood is the spirit of the world. Beside life defiled by the lust of the flesh, it places a life animated by the conviction, that the body is a temple of God; beside human beings mad upon the delights of the eye,[1] it establishes a people to show forth the praises of God;[2] and beside a world in which men are either oppressors or oppressed, it forms a living

[1] Jer. iv. 38, 'Mad upon their idols.'   [2] 1 Pet. ii. 9.

brotherhood, who bear each other's burdens, and find their glory in ministering to the ignorant and the poor.

What is the immediate and inevitable result of such a contrast? What, to the world it seeks to reclaim, is this first contact of the gospel? I have answered the question by the very terms of my description. The light which enables us to see the evil, condemns the evil on which it falls. The holy lives of Christian men and women shed a melancholy visibility on the unholy conduct of those who are ignorant of Christ. The very sacrifices of love which Christians make, bring into terrible prominence the cruel heartlessness of those for whom they are made. The love displays the hatred. The purity brings the impurity into view. Christ's prayer on the cross amid the very enemies for whom He prayed; Paul's proclamation of the known God in the presence of self-satisfied Athenian ignorance; John's practice of love beside a world to whom the love seemed strange: these contacts of light and darkness are something more than contrasts. Wherever life flashes its light on life empty of light, it carries, by the mere light it sheds, a power of condemnation. The darkness becomes a viler thing by the presence of the light. The more God's blessing is seen resting on the one, the more clearly His curse appears resting on the other. A consciousness of an evil state begins to work in the heart of the evil. God opens His book, and the dead thing ceases to be dead. 'When the law came, sin revived.' A spirit enters into the evil, and it stands upon its feet, and shakes itself, and feels and announces its real form. And thus the gospel, by the very light it sheds, becomes condemnation to the world. The book which conveys to men the tidings of salvation, is first of all to them a book of doom. It reveals God's wrath resting upon their lives. Its light places in awful contrast the evil of ungodliness. It puts a marked division between the temple and 'the court that is without the temple,' and announces to the world itself that it is lying in wickedness before God.

III.

THE DARKNESS HATING THE LIGHT.

'There is one more way in which the law contributes to evince the malignant quality of sin,—viz., it irritates into hostile activity the corrupt principles in the soul, somewhat like the case of the demoniacs in the presence of our Lord. Those principles might have their dwelling and operation there in a certain kind of deadly calm, if let alone; but let their mortal opposite come near them, and then they are provoked to reaction and rage. Rebels left undisturbed may settle into a comparative quiet; but when the rightful claimant to authority approaches, they instantly rush to arms.'— JOHN FOSTER.

BUT this is only the first foreshadowing of doom, —the indication that a curse is already resting on the wicked, rather than the infliction of new retribution. From this point onward, however, the shadow must disappear, or darken into positive increase of guilt. The imperative condition of contact with the truth is acceptance or hatred. We cannot walk by its side, and remain unaffected by it. There must be acquiescence, and through that, blessing; or rejection, and thereby, descent into deeper condemnation. Christ comes to us with new life, or new judgment. We believe, and are drawn up into the new life. We refuse to believe, and are plunged into deadlier sin. If the truth do not destroy the evil in our lives, it will excite it into fierce vitality.

This is the real secret of persecution. The world into which the truth comes is the world 'where also our Lord was crucified.' The men of this world begin by rejecting the truth, and end by dragging it before kings and councils to destroy it. First, the witnesses lift up their voice for Christ: then, the evil that underlies the world—'the beast that ascendeth out of the bottomless pit'—the Satan who is a liar and murderer from the beginning—makes war against the witnesses, and kills them.[1] The rejection becomes hatred: the hatred passes into murder.

Reading the story of persecution, we are usually moved by the sufferings of the martyrs. Our blood runs cold as we think of blameless priests and innocent women thrown to the lions, or burned, or led to stakes amid the gathering tides of the sea. But we miss the thought of a more awful doom. They that take the sword perish by the sword. The persecutor draws his sword to destroy God's witnesses. But by a more terrible weapon— the sword of divine vengeance—he brings on himself a destruction to which the sufferings of the martyrs are as nothing.

I could select no illustration of this nearly so complete, as the history of the treatment endured by our Lord. Our Lord is himself the antitype of 'the two witnesses,' and of all witnesses for the truth. The opposition encountered by Him is the type of all the opposition encountered by the gospel. And to see how in every age

[1] 'And when they shall have finished their testimony, the beast that ascendeth out of the bottomless pit shall make war against them, and shall overcome them, and kill them.'—Rev. xi. 8.

those who reject this truth are hurried by their rejection into deeper condemnation, we only require to study the history of the enmity which gathered around himself. It is John who has preserved for us the fullest history of the opposition to the Lord. One of the main designs of his Gospel, indeed, is the portrayal of the conflict between Christ and his foes.[1] Turning, therefore, to this Gospel, to acquaint ourselves with this increase of condemnation on the children of darkness, we are struck at once with the fact, that the people who began by refusing to receive the Lord, ended by putting Him to death. We see the opposition gathering like a faint cloud on the sky, deepening as the ministry of the Lord advances, until it reaches its intensest gloom in the mad rage which bursts over Pilate's chair, and spends itself in cruel mockings before the cross itself. At the outset, the element which predominates in the opposition is *incredulity*. It is the first refusal of the mind to accept a good which does not come in the accustomed channel. Who was Jesus, that he should presume to teach us? What was Nazareth, or Galilee, that we should listen to a prophet from thence? Can this man give us his flesh to eat? Is he greater than Abraham, than Jacob, than the prophets? Let him announce his greatness, if he be, by a sign from heaven. The people are at the doorways of the truth, but refuse to enter. And failing

---

[1] 'To the elucidation of this—the tracing its progress step by step, the showing its increasing virulence amidst the blameless innocence and holy words and deeds of the Redeemer—does John especially devote the middle and principal section of his Gospel.'—ALFORD, vol. i. p. 60.

to enter, they fall back. It is a deciding moment for all who hear. The true seekers find 'Him of whom Moses in the law, and the prophets, did write:' the untrue go back, and walk no more with Him. They see the light—see the wonders of the light—see even Lazarus rising from his sepulchre—yet go 'their way' towards worse iniquity.

And this worse iniquity soon begins to declare itself. As the history of the opposition advances, we find ourselves amid words of a more sullen import. The incredulity has passed into fear; the fear into hatred. The element which predominates now is *self-interest*. The 'craft' is in danger. The old ways, the familiar honours, the power and position of the existing state of things, would be disturbed, and must be given up, if Christ prevail. Christ must therefore be put down. Ominous whispers, breaking into black accusations, are bandied about, and flung in His teeth. 'The man is mad. His record of himself is false. He is a deceiver of the people.' The synagogue is closed against His disciples. 'He is a Samaritan, a demoniac, a blasphemer.' At last, the very manifestations of His divine power and holiness are ascribed to Satan. One day a poor demoniac was brought to Him, and He healed him.[1] He did this work of mercy openly. The common people were amazed. But the leaders of the people—the Pharisees—when they heard of it, said, 'It is by Beelzebub, the prince of the devils,' he has done it. This was wilful blindness and perversity. Deliberately, knowingly, they blasphemed

---

[1] Not included in John's Gospel. See Matt. xii. 22–32, and the parallel passages in Mark and Luke.

the life. With conscious purpose of soul, they called the good 'evil,' and the evil 'good.' Work done by the power of the Holiest, and in His spirit—the spirit of love and mercy—they ascribed to the devil. In this direction they could go no further in wickedness. This was the wickedness of wickedness; that dread sin, of which our Lord had to say, 'It shall not be forgiven, neither in this world, neither in the world to come.'

The last manifestations of their enmity are but the filling up of this. They have hardened themselves against the truth, and are now gnashing at it with their teeth. The spirit of the false witness passes into that of the murderer. The husbandmen say, 'This is the heir; come now, let us kill him.' Their enmity henceforward is mad rage and cruelty. And treachery and falsehood, and Jewish law and Roman power, are taxed to accomplish their murderous designs. I see my Lord standing at a Roman judgment-seat, and not as judge, but criminal. I see His blessed flesh lacerated with the scourge. I see Him mocked and spit upon. I see Him fainting under the weight of His cross. I see Him toiling up the sides of Calvary. I see Him, torn and wounded, hanging on the tree. And all along this path of pain and ignominy, I see justice and human pity drowned in falsehood and angry tumult. I see the clenched fists, the scowling looks, the savage hatred of His foes. 'O cruel and unthankful mankind, that offered such measure to the Lord of life! O infinitely merciful Saviour, that would suffer all this for unthankful mankind! That fiends should do these things to guilty souls, it is, though terrible, yet just; but that men should do this to the blessed Son of

God, it is beyond the capacity of our horror.'[1] It would not advance my illustration, to linger on the cruelty of His foes. We have seen the enmity of those who rejected Jesus, from its first beginnings to its close. We have seen this guilt showing itself at the outset as incredulity, then as selfish fear and hatred, at last as murderous and fiendish cruelty. And thus, a second time, the open book is a book of doom. He who was thus entreated in the house of His friends, was the world's life. He came revealing life, offering the life He revealed. He came, shedding along all the path He trod the beauty of this life. His deeds were the life going forth in blessings on mankind. The sorrowing saw Him, and were comforted. The weary came near to Him, and were refreshed. Yet this very boon of life, this great light of glad tidings for a sick and dying world, this book displaying the life and mercy of Heaven, was the occasion, to those who rejected it, of a fiercer condemnation. How true are the words of Christ, ' For judgment I am come into this world, that they which see not might see, and *that they which see might be made blind.*'[2]

[1] Bishop Hall.   [2] John ix. 39.

IV.

OUTER DARKNESS.

'If Jesus Christ had come only for the purpose of redemption, the whole of Scripture, and all things else, would have co-operated to that end; and nothing would have been easier than to convince infidels. As, however, He came for a stone of stumbling and rock of offence, we cannot overcome their obduracy. But this is no argument against the truth of our sentiments, since we maintain that it is agreeable to the whole course of the divine dispensation, that no conviction shall be produced in the minds of the self-willed, and those who are not sincere seekers of truth.'—PASCAL.

COME now to the closing chapter in this sad history of guilt. When persecutors have come the length of putting the witnesses of the truth to death, it seems to them, for the moment, as if victory were completely on their side. They have killed the witnesses, and are rejoicing over the dead bodies. Yet at the very moment of their triumph, they are on the eve of a more entire defeat. The truth they have persecuted enters now on a new and higher phase of its history. Man's hour is past: God's hour comes on. It is the hour of the resurrection of the truth. Strong though the grave is, it cannot retain either the Lord or His truth. The witnesses die, but it is that they may rise to a nobler and larger life. The very Calvary is the gateway into the new heavens and earth.

The truth proclaimed by the witnesses makes its new appeal in the power of an endless life. The principles of the open book are now the food of multitudes. They go to and fro on the earth, and lay hold on the universal thought and life of man. The very air seems full of them. Like the lightning, the truth gleams from east to west over all the heavens. It is no longer a solitary thinker, a prophet, a reformer; it is a CAUSE. Christ has ascended, but His Church is on the earth. Luther is dead, but Protestantism is knocking at every door. The new cause speaks to men as an ambassador of the Lord. It claims instant and complete adhesion, instant and complete surrender of evil, from men and nations. It lays its obligations on churches, customs, and laws, and on all public and private life. There can be no halting between two opinions now. He that is not with the truth is against it. But on him who is against it, the Anathema Maranatha descends.

In these new circumstances, the progress of the truth is a continued process of disintegration and separation. The truth detaches from the world everything that is weary of evil ways, and attaches to itself everything that sympathizes with its principles. By the very withdrawal of worth from the world, the bulk of goodness is increased, and the evil in the world is at the same time driven back into a worse and more hopeless state. The good becomes better; the bad, worse.

It is not, and in this probation state it never can be, a perceptible process. The separation advances in the deeps, where only the eye of God can penetrate. On the surface of society, men mingle as before. It is at the springs of their being they divide. The tares and the wheat grow together till the harvest. Often, when we seem to detect the separation, our inferences are wrong. Good men appear to side with evil-doers, as when they call in question the authority of some venerable superstition. Bad men appear to take part with the righteous, as when they clamour for liberty of conscience. And often also, when the struggle is for particular principles, men who are really at one will seem to be opposed. But at every point, and under every aspect of the struggle, and beneath all the seeming unity or confusion of the surface, the conflict marches, with inevitable step, towards a complete and irreversible separation of the righteous and the wicked.

Christ's cause comes into a world overgrown with evil, and the battle it wages has to traverse every inch of the field. It is a necessary consequence, that one truth will be more prominent in one generation, and a different truth in the next. But this only secures a more entire sifting of souls, and a deeper and wider separation. To every soul who hears it, the gospel comes with its 'generation truth,' and submits the choice of adhesion to Christ in the interest of that truth, or adhesion to Christ's enemies to oppose it. In the light of the particular truth which lies nearest the needs of his age, he is asked to adhere to Christ, or to separate from Him.

Look for a moment at the history of the Christian Church. To a great extent it has been a history of conflict for the kingly, priestly, and prophetic offices of her divine Head. Against the kingly power of the world, during the earlier centuries of her career, the Church had to maintain the claim of the kingship of Christ. In the middle ages, against the priestly claims of the Papal Church, she had to lift up her testimony for His priesthood. And in our own day, her principal contest is with the philosophy and thought which refuse to receive Him as God's prophet for the world. Now, along the entire path of those successive conflicts, a process of separation has gone on. Men have had to arrange themselves on the side of Christ, or against Him; to accept the truth of His kingship in the ages when that was contended for; or of His priesthood and prophetic functions when these came to be maintained. And the separation thus effected, goes on through every generation, and for every individual of every generation, and for eternity as well as time. And thus the gospel, which came to unite, becomes, by the resistance of its enemies, a divider. For eternity, it gathers the lambs into the fold of the Shepherd, and repels the impenitent to a greater distance from God. It fills the mansions of heaven with the countless multitudes of the blessed, and it determines the doom of those who are to be turned into hell. And for time, at every advancing step in its sublime career, it renders the position of the unbeliever more untenable. As it dispels the darkness of the world, and advances its victorious banner, men have less and less excuse for abiding in error. The blessings it dispenses, the life it communicates, the power it imparts, are open to every eye. The men who shall resist it now, must resist with a high hand and a deliberate will, and in the very interests of untruth. And so, we are told, it will be. 'In the last days, men shall be lovers of their own selves, covetous, boasters, proud, blasphemers, disobedient to parents, unthankful, unholy, without natural affection, truce-breakers, false accusers, incontinent, fierce, despisers of those that are good, traitors, heady, high-minded, lovers of pleasures more than lovers of God; having a form of godliness, but denying the power thereof.'[1] As the coming of the Lord draws near, this mystery of iniquity may change its outward aspects and shapes; may put on new robes, or re-deck itself in the cast-off garments of dead iniquities; or it may array itself as an angel of light; but, beneath all its disguises and displays, it is only fulfilling its gloomy destiny, and reaping, for all who sow to it, deterioration and descent into blacker unrighteousness. From generation to generation it retreats further from the truth; it becomes a more malignant incarnation of evil, until at last the awful reality underlying the crowded surface of mankind shall be two diverse and repellent worlds: on the one side, the world of Christian truth and life, glorious with the glory of the latter days, pure, spotless, and unwrinkled; and on the other, the world of sin and error, the heir of all the wickedness which has ever been,[2] a multitude of human beings empty of every germ of good, driven from every principle of righteousness, wholly and irreclaimably

---

[1] 2 Tim. iii. 1-5.

[2] 'That upon you may come all the righteous blood shed upon the earth, from the blood of righteous Abel unto the blood' of the last martyr for the truth.—Matt. xxiii. 35. 'The fellowship of sin and punishment before God's judgment actually extends thus far, even to the descending connection of growing corruption, as is seen in a people, when the children, not warned by the guilt of their fathers, continue it, and carry it to its consummation.'—STIER.

evil,—the last, fiercest, most daring embodiment of the everchanging antichrist. And then the separation shall indeed be complete, and as irreversible as complete. On the one side, the followers of the Lamb; on the other, the followers of the beast. *Within,* 'they that do His commandments, that have right to the tree of life; *without*, dogs, and sorcerers, and whoremongers, and murderers, and idolaters, and whosoever loveth and maketh a lie.'[1]

When a Roman general was decreed a triumph, and entered the imperial city at the head of his victorious army, the altars smoked with incense, and incense-bearers filled the air with fragrance. Behind the conqueror came the prisoners he had taken in war. Of those prisoners, some had accepted the laws of the empire, and were destined for honours; some had refused submission, and were doomed to die. When the magnificent procession arrived at the Capitol, the doomed captives were withdrawn and conducted to the place of death; the others remained with the hero to share in his triumph. To those two bands of prisoners, how different the fragrance which filled the air! To the first, it came all sweetened with the certainty of life; to the last, it was a breath of sadness and the grave.

Thus, in its twofold issues, advances the cause of Jesus. He comes up out of the wilderness of conflict 'perfumed with myrrh and frankincense.'[2] He triumphs and rides forth gloriously, leading His captives in His train. The lives of His people,—their graces, their holy influences,—are the fragrance which proclaims His

[1] Rev. xxii. 14, 15.   [2] Song of Songs iii. 6.

triumph. Blessed, and ever blessed, are they who have allowed this King to conquer, who have become captives by their own will to His law. To them, the new life which breathes from their own spirits, and all the influences and manifestations of grace in others by their side, are a foretaste of yet higher blessings, a fragrant incense of heaven itself. But to them who refuse His authority, and in the face of all His urgency will not have Him for their king, the very blessings which announce the conquests of His grace are a 'savour of death unto death.'[1]

[1] 'Now thanks be unto God, who always causeth us to triumph in Christ, and maketh manifest the savour of His knowledge by us in every place. For we are unto God a sweet savour of Christ, in them that are saved, and in them that perish. To the one we are the savour of death unto death; and to the other the savour of life unto life.'—2 Cor. ii. 14-16.

'Θριαμβεύειν (which is mistranslated in A. V.) means *to lead a man as a captive in a triumphal procession;* Θριαμβεύειν ἐν Χριστῷ means *to lead captive in a triumph over the enemies of Christ.* The metaphor is taken from the triumphal procession of a victorious general. God is celebrating His triumph over His enemies. St Paul (who had been so great an opponent of the gospel) is a captive following in the train of the triumphal procession; yet (at the same time, by a characteristic change of metaphor) an incense-bearer, scattering incense (which was always done on these occasions) as the procession moves on. Some of the conquered enemies were put to death when the procession reached the Capitol: to them the smell of the incense was *an odour of death ending in death;* to the rest who were spared, *an odour of life ending in life.* The metaphor appears to have been a favourite one with Paul; it occurs again, Col. ii. 15.'—CONYBEARE AND HOWSON.

Part Third.

DISCIPLINE;

OR,

REVELATIONS OF WRATH ON THE WAY OF LIFE.

'Christ's soul must needs descend into hell before it ascended into heaven. So must also the soul of man. When a man truly perceiveth and considereth himself, who and what he is, and findeth himself utterly vile, and wicked, and unworthy of all the comfort and kindness that he hath ever received from God, or from the creatures, he falleth into such a deep debasement and despising of himself, that he thinketh himself unworthy that the earth should bear him, and it seemeth to him reasonable that all creatures in heaven and earth should rise up against him, and avenge their Creator on him, and should punish and torment him. It seemeth to him that he shall be eternally lost and damned, and a footstool to all the devils in hell, and that this is right and just, and all too little compared to his sins, which he so often and in so many ways hath committed against God his Creator. He who in this present time entereth into this hell, entereth afterward into the kingdom of heaven and obtaineth a foretaste thereof, which excelleth all the delight and joy which he ever hath had, or could have, in this present time from temporal things.'

Theologica Germanica.

'When the beloved disciple took the angel's little open book,
Which by the Lord's command he ate, it tasted bitter after sweet.
What sweetness does the promise yield, when by the Spirit's power sealed!
The longing soul is filled with good, nor feels a wish for other food.
By these inviting tastes allured, we pass to what must be endured;
For soon we find it is decreed, that bitter must to sweet succeed.
When sin revives and shows its power, when Satan threatens to devour,
When God afflicts and men revile, we draw our steps with pain and toil.'

Olney Hymn.

I.

IN THE DEEPS.

'Woe is me! for I am undone.'

AT this point it may be well—between our study of the two books of providence, and the books of the final judgment—to clear out a little space for the discussion of the place, which the element of wrath has in the processes of redemption. What we have hitherto, and perhaps too abundantly seen, is, that 'wrath is revealed from heaven against all ungodliness and unrighteousness of men.' But the course of our study has permitted us to look at that wrath exclusively as an instrument of doom. Is there no other end which its revelation subserves? Is it always and only for destruction it is revealed? May it not sometimes be a fire of cleansing rather than of burning—a discipline more than a punishment? And are there not circumstances, in which it is revealed to advance the people of God on the path of life; and when it is, in relation to them, but the other side of love?

We are familiar with the statement, that Christ's people ascend to the kingdom through tribulation. But we leave out a large portion of its meaning when we limit, as we sometimes do, the tribulation to physical suffering and persecution. Of necessity, it must mean far more than that. It is, as often as otherwise, actual sight, or experience of Christ's wrath. From earth to heaven is to every one, more or less, through wrath to love. We ourselves consciously appeal to wrath in the most loving work in which we can be engaged. 'Knowing the terror of the Lord, we persuade men.' Love beckons the soul; but the path we tread, passes at appointed stages through the fires of wrath.

The spiritual history of every generation to which the life of Christ is offered, is the story of two crowds travelling on opposite paths: the one, through rejection of that life, to endless wrath; the other, through experiences of disciplinary wrath, to endless and full possession of the life. For the one crowd, there is wrath at the end of the journey; for the other, wrath by the way. It is this 'wrath by the way' whose revelations I propose at present to unfold. I mean to confine myself to the history of a single generation. Keeping in view, on the one hand, the purpose of the gospel, and on the other, the accordance and growth in that purpose of those to whom it has been revealed, I intend to trace the development of this purpose along the spiritual career of one generation; and along this track, to show, that in the progressive movements of the providence of grace, and in the successive stages of our common instruction in righteousness, there is, at every stage, a new and appropriate revelation of wrath.

It is, indeed, only a limited view of the work of discipline which by this method can be displayed. It is to follow Christ's footsteps across only one field of His infinitely extended operations. We are to witness Him laying bare the handwriting of His anger before the hearts and consciences of but one generation of His people. But in this science, the little contains the great. From His dealings with one generation, under the Christian dispensation, and by the instruments of Christian life, we may learn His dealings with all.

In the purpose of redemption, as it evolves in any one generation, four special ends may be distinguished. There is, first of all, the conviction of sin; then, conversion from sin; then, chastisement for sin; then, separation from surrounding sin. What I am now to show, is a revelation of wrath intertwined with the outworking of each of these ends. Four movements of the Lord in His redemptive function: and side by side with these, four experiences of His wrath by the redeemed.

Let us select, then, a single generation. Let it be our own. Let the world be conceived of under its ordinary condition. The currents of life, I shall suppose, are flowing in the familiar channels. Men are busy as ants, and with no higher purpose. They are abroad in markets, warehouses, factories, fields, and ships. The farmer is sowing. The landlord is preserving his game. The member of Parliament is addressing his constituents. The councillor is discussing the affairs of the city. The soldier is proving the last Armstrong cannon. The rifleman is studying the next change in his dress. Up in the attic, poor Mary is competing, through the long hours of the night, with the merciless sewing-machine. Down in the cellar, poor Tom is sweating his life out in unwholesome toil. In the pits, and at the blazing furnaces, the slaves of the mine are labouring like machines.

Amid the poisonous exhalations of chemical works, human lungs are being rotted out, and old age precipitated on men who have not spent half their years. In every direction, pulling down and building up proceed as in the days of old. And outside of the work spheres, it is the same familiar scene of ordinary times: 'eating and drinking; marrying and giving in marriage.' Busy vanity is chasing its butterfly. Busy idleness is producing its mischiefs. Busy care is darkening its casket. The houses are ringing with laughter, or drenched in tears. The pleasure party and the burial party pass each other on the streets. And little children, just as in the days of our fathers, are hurrying forth, some to play, some to the school, and some, alas, to the dreary education of the factory.

But what strange feeling is this, which on a sudden sweeps over that chequered scene? Why those groups upon the street; and those earnest gatherings at night in upper rooms? What has filled the empty seats of the prayer-meeting with anxious worshippers, and imparted to the dullest sermon in the church an interest, which the freshest formerly failed to inspire? Why, especially, those fierce agonies and unspeakable emotions in the very audience and eye of the assembled crowds? What wrings the heart of that quiet maiden, of that well-conditioned youth, of that church-going parent, of old and young, of good and bad, in assemblies and in solitude? Why do they cry out in their prayers, as if hell had let loose its terrors? It is because hell has actually been let loose upon their souls. 'The pains of hell' have found them out. They are smitten by the first shocks of a revival. The shadow of God's wrath is lying heavy upon them : convictions of unrepented sin are agonizing them. Their prostrations and cries are foretastes, sent to them in mercy, of the terrors of the day of judgment.

It is a revelation of wrath : the first display, in the development of the redemption purpose, of Christ's wrath against sin. He would save this generation : He begins by laying bare to them the terrors of His wrath. The life of the generation hitherto has transacted itself behind refuges of custom, and sense, and error ; and even at best was but a round of external duties. His wrath was burning hot against it, was burning hot within it ; but the poor, preoccupied, careless, world-bedimmed life, felt it not, beheld it not. On it went, with this screen of delusion between itself and the awful reality. On it might have gone for ever, behind the same wall of peril. But now the screen is suddenly withdrawn. The hail has destroyed the refuges of lies. The gracious Saviour has sent forth the Spirit. The soul is brought face to face with the realities of judgment. The soul stands naked in the presence of the Judge. There is no refuge, no screen, no delusion any more. Conscience is confronted with the open page of the divine law. Conscience and the law ! 'Oh, mercy ! mercy for a poor, undone sinner ! mercy for one who has never, never lived to the glory of God !' Such are the cries of the convicted soul. And these cries are simply prelusions of the last awful cry : 'Mountains, fall on us; rocks, hide us from the wrath of the Lamb.' And they are evoked by the same spectacle. The brightness of His coming has unsealed the book, and over the entire life of the sin-spotted generation is seen written the awful words, 'The end of these things is death.' 'Hitherto,' said one who was saved in one of those revival visitations, 'Hitherto I have been as a man travelling along a bridge; and in a moment the bridge was swept away from under me, and I found myself sinking into the roaring stream.'

'Oh, mother,' said a second who was smitten by the Spirit, 'you tell me what I need to see is hell. I *have* seen hell. I have seen into the very bottom of hell. I see nothing but hell. I am in hell.' And so, in a sense, he was. He and that other awoke to find themselves lost, sinking into the roaring gulph, in the hands of a God they had despised, and filled and encompassed with the revelation of His wrath. 'Destruction from the Almighty!' exclaims the great Howe, addressing sinners; 'what a terror must that be to you! To eat and drink under wrath! To buy and sell, to plough and sow, and all under wrath! And with a curse from God covering you as a garment, cleaving to you as a curse, flowing as oil into your bones, mingling with all your affairs and all your comforts, with whatsoever you do, and whatsoever you enjoy! And to be all the while upon the brink of eternity, and not, for aught you know, to have an handbreadth—not, more than a breath between you and eternal woes!'[1] To see all this, to feel it in connection with one's own soul and well-being,—vividly to experience what is thus portrayed, is conviction of sin. And conviction of sin is the first revelation of Christ's wrath in the history of a soul's redemption.

[1] Sermon on *Reconciliation between God and Man.*

II.

BENEATH THE CROSS.

'The chastisement of our peace was upon Him.'

THE second revelation of wrath takes place when, to the convinced and anxious sinners of the generation, the way of peace is opened up through the death of Christ. 'Christ crucified' is a revelation of love. But it is a revelation of wrath as well. It is not all love which meets the eye in that spectacle. There is love, but there is also wrath. It is love shining through wrath; love reaching over wrath. The glory around the brow of the love is the wrath endured.

Consider the really arresting and peace-giving element in the cross. It is the sight of the wrath, which the roused conscience discovers in the hour of conviction, transferred to the person of another. On the head of Him who knew no sin, the trembling sinner is made to see the retributions of sin descending. He beholds an innocent Saviour in the sinner's place on that tree. He sees Him wounded for our transgressions, and bruised for our iniquities. The wounds and the bruises which we deserved, He has intercepted on their way to us.

Ah, wounded head, must Thou endure such shame and scorn!
The blood is trickling from Thy brow, pierced by the crown
of thorn.

. . . . .

Ah, Lord, Thy woes belong, Thy cruel pains to me!
The burden of my sin and wrong hath all been laid on Thee![1]

Wonderful, therefore, though it may sound, the book of judgment is unsealed in the cross. On that cross, Christ submits to be written over with our doom. In His own flesh, He receives the awful handwriting of wrath. For our sakes, that we might be redeemed from sin, He wrapped himself round with sin. He inscribed the doom of sin on His own life and flesh. He actually became the book. This is the startling fact. While He hung on that cross, He was the book written without and within; the revelation to man of God's judgments upon sin; the living, conscious, willing parchment on which the wrath of Heaven was written. Those nail-marks in the hands?—They are letters of the book. Those blood-rills on the brow?—They are letters of the book. That travail of His soul?—It is the very essence of the book. Within and without, in His spirit and on His flesh, the book is laid bare.

O book full of mystery! O book to put all mystery away! Book 'held in the hands of the Lamb!' Book penned by the hands which suffered! Book written in the blood which atoned! Book of wrath, yet written over with the entreaties of love! Book of love, yet inscribed with the revelations of wrath!

The holy person of Christ is here all marked and marred with the gashes and scars of sin. Along that

[1] Paul Gerhardt.

immortal frame, death-fires are shooting. Over that pure spirit, death's mists are gathering. It is the unsealed book I see. But this time it has been opened, not to terrify, but to win; not to fill the hearts of sinners with anguish, but with peace; not to give foretastes of the doom which awaits them, but to tell them of escape from that doom. It is still a revelation of wrath, but it is given, to lead sinners out from all terror, and dispeace, and sin: out along the path consecrated by the blood, and into the refuge and home of the soul in the heart of the sufferer.

III.

PERFECTING HOLINESS.

'In a little wrath I hid my face from thee for a moment.'

THE next revelation of judgment comes by chastisement. But at this point, the life of the generation whose spiritual career we are following, must be conceived of as parting into two different channels. Of those who are smitten by the first sight of Christ's wrath,—the sight of it revealed in the hour of conviction,—only a few go forward to find the second revelation of it, when it is displayed in the cross. Even of those who see it on the cross, some turn aside and walk no more with Christ. Ruth comes Christ's way; Orpah goes back to Moab. It is to those who come Christ's way—the really converted ones—I restrict my attention at present.

These enter upon a life of discipline. The conditions of life are now the endurance of sorrow and the conflict with sin. By trials and crosses they learn subjection to their Father's will. What I want to show is, that these crosses and sufferings are a revelation of judgment.

Let us bethink ourselves of the words with which Christians are stirred up, to co-operate with Christ in the work of their redemption. They are words steeped in the shadows of the judgment-day. The very words made use of to express the revelation of wrath in the cross, are applied to this process of discipline. The Christian is to 'crucify the old man with his lusts.' He is 'to mortify the deeds of the flesh:' that is to say, he is to put God's stamp of death on every evil in his heart, and to go on stamping, and destroying, and casting out, until 'the old man' within him is utterly and for ever put away. But this is just judgment upon sin. There is indeed love in it, and growth in it, and therein this process of chastisement differs from punishment, which is simply and only wrath; but there is here also, as in the cross, a mixture of wrath with the love. It is Christ's wrath on the sins of His flock. We are not made perfect in a day. Conversion is only the turning towards the light. We carry about with us after conversion hidden and undeveloped sins. These live and work through all our thoughts and actions, and would destroy us, if left alone. They are the sleeping serpents we have nestled in our breasts. But Christ treads upon the lion and the adder wherever He finds them.[1] The young lion and the dragon He tramples under feet. He is related to the sins of His people precisely

---

[1] 'For convincing a man of judgment by the gospel . . . he must understand, that upon righteousness received by faith, judgment shall follow, on the one hand, to the destroying the works of the devil in the believer, and to the perfecting the work of sanctification with power; and that upon refusing to take righteousness by faith in Jesus Christ, judgment shall follow, on the other hand, to the condemnation of the misbeliever, and destroying of him with Satan and his servants for ever.'—*Practical Use of Saving Knowledge.*

as He is related to the sins of His enemies. He is utterly, irreconcilably opposed to them. His wrath is thus the safety of His people. He has come into the world to destroy the works of the devil. His destructions do not falter when they come to the lives of Christian men and women. The devils must be cast out. He brings His people into circumstances where the secret sins begin to tell. The hidden lust, or doubt, or habit comes out of its inner chamber, and steps upon the house-top; and the vile affection, the scarlet sin, is laid bare. Oh, Thou who searchest the hearts of men, how much need we all have to cry, Cleanse us from secret sins! Search us, and try us, and see if there be any wicked way in us. We are all overrun with wicked ways. The evil thing is in our hearts, and we suspect it not. Because we have seen that Christ has died for us, we take no further care. We sing our song on the banks of the Red Sea, and challenge the future to find us untrue to Christ. We say to the misgiving fear, 'Is thy servant a dog, that he should do such a thing?' We build ourselves up in self-esteem. If the Lord were to let us alone in this state, we would perish. But, blessed be His name, He will not let us alone. He takes us to some Marah or other, and the pent-up murmurs, the distrust, the weariness of the way, break out. He takes us to the door of the hall of judgment, and to the scrutiny of idle women, and the coiled-up denial hisses out, with oaths and curses, 'I know not the man.' Ah, Israel! Ah, Peter! You did not know your hearts. But lo! now the seal is unloosed, and the page is laid bare, and the black handwriting of sin is displayed; and along with that, intertwined with that, in the agony of your conscience, or in the drying up of your bodily moisture, or in the rending of ties by bereavement, or in the loss of means, or name, or liberty, the fiery letters of the consuming fire are revealed, twining and burning, twining and burning, until the black words are effaced from the life, and the child is made perfect through suffering. *Our* God is a consuming fire.

IV.

CONTENDING WITH WRONG.

> 'Men groan from out of the city, and the soul of the wounded crieth out.'

BUT the instruction of His people in righteousness is not completed, when they are made to see by His chastisements the evil which is in themselves. There is yet another field of evil, on which their efforts must be turned, and against which His wrath is burning. This will introduce us to a fourth unsealing of the book. Besides the evil which has had its root and increase in the individual lives of Christ's people, there is the evil which is round about them; the evil which was at work before they entered the world; the evil of circumstances and laws and customs which they were born into, with which their only connection may have been the connection of neighbourhood, or acquiescence, or silence.

I do not require to prove, that the responsibility of Christ's people does not terminate at the evils of their individual hearts. It reaches over to the extinction of all evil. The function of the Christian is the eradication of evil from the earth. He is here to declare against it, to war with it, to destroy it. He is to carry Christian truth and principle into every domain of human life— into thought, science, laws, habits, societies. If he discovers, standing out from himself, or intertwined with his own relationships, a domain of life possessed by unchristian principle, by falsehood, by devilishness, beside that evil he is not free to live in peace. That is seed of the serpent; he is seed of the truth. Acquiescence is sin. Silence is sin. No matter how delicately wrought the garments of the evil may be, how intimately inwoven with existing interests its practices may be, the vocation of the Christian is to put it to death. It is the Agag of the moment. The Christian is the Samuel who must hew it in pieces before his Lord.

Stated in this general and unapplied way, the responsibility is universally admitted. But unhappily, the eye which has been long accustomed to an evil, living in the midst of it, familiar with it as a thing handed down from father to son, cognizant of the threads of good which have been twined around it, does not easily see it to be a thing which must be destroyed. It is an unrighteous trade, I shall suppose; but then, righteous men are connected with it; righteous families are supported by it; and, down at a certain level, righteous ends are subserved by it. Or it is an oppressive system; but then, our fathers submitted to it, and honourable men are the administrators of it, and honourable work has been accomplished by it. The films of custom and familiarity blind us to the wickedness.

There is here, in consequence, another field on which Christ must display His anger. In among all those embodiments of evil, He must flash the glances of the consuming fire. He must open yet another page of the judgment-book.

The two evils I am to refer to are so recent and well known, that I may content myself with the briefest statement of them. The retribution on the one is past and completed; the retribution on the other is going on. The one was an evil in commercial law, the other is an evil in social life.

We are all old enough to remember the termination of the restrictive laws on corn. The history of these laws is the history of a continuous revelation of divine wrath. No sooner were they enacted, than their malign course began to be traceable in disastrous effects upon society. Originating at first in the selfishness of class hearts, they received their authentication in the enactments of class legislation. The evil seemed but a little thing at the beginning—a mere speck in the heavens, a thing of little import: but by and by the heavens were made dark by it; it shut out sun and star; it shut out God. In the bitterness of those who suffered by it, the sorrowful cry went up, Can there be a God in the heavens, and such a law allowed upon the earth? The cloud gathered. The evil influences began to tell. Entire trades were laid prostrate. The industry of the nation was cramped. Down came the malign thing, cold and chilling in its influence. Down it fell upon thought, upon energy, upon hope, upon capital, upon labour, upon the Church itself. Heavier and increasing in violence as it fell, it descended through the entire mass of the social system, corrupting the cements of society, filtering into the homes of the toiling myriads, soaking to the lowest basement, trickling out in the cellars and hovels of the poorest poor, oozing through their little comforts, damping their little joys, until their very bodies caught the influence, and became clammy with the sweat of disease and death. These were the natural results of the evil; but they were something more. They were revelations of God's anger against it. And thoughtful men became more cognizant of the anger, as the results took on still darker hues.

What was the significance of the scenes which preceded and hastened the downfall of these laws? Mothers were seen cowering in unnatural sadness over their newborn babes, whose coming they felt to be only an increase of woe. Fathers were seen rushing out from the sufferings they did not cause, to slake their vengeance in public crime. The fires of the incendiary flung up their lurid horrors on the sky. And the joy of all the land was parched.—It was Christ laying bare His wrath. It was Christ descending through human sufferings and wrongs, to confront those of His people who had social or political influence, with an evil, in the presence of which they were silently, and unprotestingly, living; and to arouse them,—by these flashes of His anger,—to stand up in His name and power, and demand the abolition of the pernicious law.

Take another instance. Look at the condition of the very poor in the large towns and cities of the kingdom. It is still something frightful to think of; but twenty or thirty years ago, the evil was as great, and no man cared for it. Living in the same community, under the same laws, within the same jurisdiction, at our very doors, they lived in a world different from our own. In a country noted for its education, they were uneducated. In cities noted for their piety, they were heathens. In fected by evil habits, living in apartments worse than the mud-huts of our ancestors, breathing a poisonous atmosphere, without joy, without self-respect, without room to develop, without comfort — except the comfort which pernicious stimulants could impart — without opportunity for well-doing, or proper work, or fair wages for the work they actually did, or sufficient food or clothing, or instruction, or faith, — they lived on, from January to December, under conditions which it was inhuman in the rest of us to suffer.

But Christ was not silent. He heard the cries of the wounded. And He came down to display His wrath. He took a pestilence, and gave it wings. He said to it: 'Go to and fro upon the land, until My people are roused.' And the obedient pestilence went forth. It entered cities and villages. It overshadowed the land with an oppressive gloom. It smote without distinction of rank or age. It passed, in our cities, from street to street, from stair to stair, from bed to bed. It took the women from the mill, and the companion from the bed. It left no circle without a gap; no heart without a terror; no street without a corpse; no day without a shower of death. And then it spread its wings and went away, and the heavens were clear. But only for a time. Christian men did not learn its lesson: and it came again. And then again it disappeared, but only to return. And it will return again, and yet again, until Christ's people, following the footsteps of a wise science, shall trace the evil back along all its tracks, and set themselves, with thoroughly earnest hearts, to separate their human brothers and sisters from the foul sewer, and the contaminated atmosphere, and the unwholesome dwelling-place, and the hardships and perils of ignorance, and drunkenness, and unpaid labour, and oppressive poverty. For the pestilence is just the revelation of the wrath of Him who hears the cry of the afflicted, and is the helper and judge of the poor, who have no helper upon earth.

V.

THE END.

'These shall go away into everlasting punishment.'

AFTER these things cometh the end. Christ's righteousness would be only half told out, and the education of His people would be incomplete, if the wisdom of those who followed, and the utter madness of those who rejected Him, or His laws, had not at last an unanswerable demonstration.

We have just seen how Christ deals with His people, to arouse them to the conflict with the evil which surrounds them. I shall now suppose that the film of familiarity is dissolved; that His people behold in all its vileness the evil thing He wants them to destroy. The trade, the custom, the unrighteous law, the ignorance, the idolatry, the lengths and breadths of unconverted, or uncared for, human life: they see them all. And they are at length aroused and go forth to the conflict. The Christian thinker is flashing out his consumption of error. The patriot is denouncing the unrighteous law. The philanthropist is down among the wretched with his charities. The missionary is out with the blessed gospel among the heathen. The kingdom of Christ has entered the field against the kingdom of the world.

The End.

But now is put forth the might of the enemy. Along the path of the Christian enterprise,—whatever that may be,—comes the tide of scorn and opposition. The good cause is hindered—is driven back. The victory hasteneth not. The fighters on the Lord's side faint and fail. The shadows gather over them and they go hence, and victory is not yet declared.

Christ is not one to stand neutral in circumstances like these. His retributions come down on the opposers,— every moment come down. But He reserves the full revelation of them for eternity. Only now and again, only here and there, at far intervals, and by mere prelusions, does He pronounce, in time, His verdict in the hearing of the contending parties.

A powerful commercial company in India lays its ban on the gospel. An ardent Carey steals out like a criminal to break through their ban. He has to shelter himself and his work under the wing of a foreign flag. He has to endure the opposition and the enmity of these merchant princes. The opposition is not ended when he dies. But Carey's successors are summoned to witness the retribution. The fire of a great mutiny travels across the land. It is very tempestuous round about![1] But in the end, the adversary—the commercial company—is dissolved, and its ban is broken for ever.

A confederacy of priestcraft and tyranny shuts out the Bible from Italy. The oppressors are sitting on their thrones in fancied security. Their oaths are broken. Their subjects are trodden beneath their hoofs. The people are perishing for lack of knowledge, and the

[1] Ps. l. 3.

knowledge is forbidden. But the iniquity has risen to the brim. There is a yearning and a movement among the nations. A spark descends from above. The pent-up wrath of the down-trodden breaks forth. They awake in awful rage, and revolution comes on the wings of the rage; and the tyrants are driven forth, and the Bible passes into the land. But vindications so immediate as these are rare. And immediate vindications are seldom complete. The day of complete vindication is the 'great day of His wrath,' when the lives of the parties in the great conflict are evolved, and their labours have had their issues in evil or in good.—To the events of this day we must now transfer our thoughts.

Imagine, then, that all the souls whose spiritual history we have been following, have received from the Great Teacher their last lesson on earth, and are now gone home to himself. The generation to which they belonged is gathered to the fathers. Other eyes look up at the beautiful heavens. Other feet tread the dusty earth. Into other hearts is poured the story of redeeming love. They are gone out of the scene of conflict. Of all the souls whom we beheld standing at the opening of the ways so shortly back, not one remains. They have passed away from 'the things which are seen' into the world of the unseen. But the verdict of the Judge on their lives is still to be declared.

In the cemetery of the Jews at Paris there is a bust by Préault, in which the head is bound up in a shroud, and a finger presses the lips. It is the figure of death. What that finger typifies must be removed. Those lips shall speak. That shroud shall be left, 'wrapped together in a place by itself' in the grave. The seal of death shall be broken; and the spiritual secrets it conceals shall be brought up into the light. The 'well done' or the 'woe' of the Judge must be pronounced on the lives of all.

It has been no part of my plan to follow out the histories of those who refused to hear the voice of the Judge. On earth they went their own way, out from the light He was offering, out into the darkness of unbelief and sin. They lived their life. They supped their Esau's mess. They went out and in, and married and were given in marriage, without the fear or the love of God in any of their ways.

And they were able to do it, because they refused to acknowledge the handwriting of wrath, which, in moments and spasms of conviction, had been revealed in their lives. Their self-made blinds concealed the facts from the eyes which had the most need to see them. They lived and lusted, they grew old and died, without awaking to the awful fact, that there is a Judge who judgeth righteously, to whom they must render an account of their lives. From them came the opposition to the truth. From them came the hatred of the cross. Their ranks supplied the men who crushed the liberties, and banned the glad tidings, and ground down the poor, and hindered the works of mercy in the generation to which they belonged.

But now their strength is departed. They are standing in the presence of the Judge. They have heard the peal of the trumpet, and are risen to the resurrection of doom. Where now are those refuges of lies behind which they excused their indifference to the truth? Where now the worth of the companions, whose smiles strengthened them in unbelief? Where now the interests, for which they cruelly hindered the cause of Christ? Where now the slanders and the vaunts, by which they taunted the humble followers of the Lamb? The hail has swept them away; and they themselves are here, naked and open, before the eyes of Him they refused.

Would it be mercy in God to suffer those enemies of His people to continue by their side? Shall the Judge of all the earth, who has seen their crooked ways, their malice, and their cruelty, and who in His people's sufferings has himself been wounded, allow the two crowds to mingle as before? Would this be just in itself? Would it be merciful towards His people? Shall *their* future be darkened as before by this cloud of evil? Must *they* for ever and ever go out and in with the men, who scorned them and persecuted them on the earth—the honest with the dishonest, the holy with the vile? At the end of all, shall there be no difference between those who accepted the gospel, and travelled along its fiery pathway, and those who rejected it, and refused that path? Yes, my brothers, there shall be difference, deep and radical, total and everlasting! 'These shall go away into everlasting punishment; but the righteous into life eternal.' The one party submitted on earth to the discipline of the 'consuming fire,' and stands now, pure and beautiful, in its resurrection splendour; the other refused to submit, and must now encounter, but not for discipline, the fire it refused. By revelations of wrath along all their journey, the people of

Christ were led up to glory. But the wrath which the loving One revealed to make them holy is now to break forth as retribution on those who would not travel by their side. By wrath prepared for the inheritance, they are now by wrath to be protected. And into their blessed society 'there shall in no wise enter anything that defileth, neither whatsoever worketh abomination, or maketh a lie.' The last revelation of wrath which Christ's people shall see, will be the revelation of the righteous judgment of God upon their enemies on the day of wrath.

'Knowing the terrors of the Lord, we persuade men.' For every soul of man, two revelations are provided: one in the cross, beaming with mercy, quick with life to him who accepts it; one in the laws and retributions of providence, dark with anger, terrible in the power of the avenger it displays. Once the two revelations flowed into one. In the pierced flesh of the Redeemer, the mercy and the wrath shone forth together. Once again they will reappear in the same conjunction, when the Son of man returns to judge the world. He will come beaming with love for His people, flashing with anger against His foes. But that anger shall quickly be absorbed in retributions. The wrath 'revealed from heaven against all ungodliness and unrighteousness of men'—the wrath displayed in the cross in the person of Christ—is displayed on His person no more. He has ceased to intercept the doom of the wicked. 'The acceptable year is ended.' 'The day of vengeance is in His heart.' The book written in His own blood is now to be inscribed with the blood of His foes. 'In that day shall the deaf hear the words of the book.'[1] The prelusions of retribution have given place to the doom they preluded. Retribution, unmixed and irreversible, has passed down into the lives and persons of the wicked. They are 'filled with their own devices.' The book, whose openings on the way of life, we have been studying—the awful revelation of God's wrath against sin—has found its last embodiment in the experiences and sufferings of the wicked. Its fiery sentences are entering into their souls. Spotted and scarred with the sins they have sinned, THEY have become the book.

We can read in it no longer. The shadows of the outer darkness are descending on its page. But out of the gloom, like the sighing and moaning of a wind at night, arises the wail of the lost.[2]

[1] Is. xxix. 18.

[2] 'Thus we passed through the filthy mixture of the spirits and the rain, with paces slow, touching a little on the future life.

'Wherefore I said, Master shall these torments increase after the great sentence, or grow less, or remain as burning?

'And he to me: Return to thy Science,* which has it that the more a thing is perfect, the more it feels pleasure, and likewise pain! Though these accursed people never attain to true perfection, yet shall they be nearer to it after than before.

'We went round that road, speaking much more than I repeat.'
   DANTE, *The Inferno*, canto vi. Dr Carlyle's Translation.

* The Aristotelian Philosophy.

Part Fourth.

THE BOOKS;

OR,

THE MEMORIES OF THE JUDGED.

'And I saw a great white throne, and Him that sat on it, from Whose face the arth and the heaven fled away; and there was found no place for them. And I saw the dead, small and great, stand before God: and the books were opened.'

John.

'I beheld till the thrones were cast down, and the Ancient of days did sit, Whose garment was white as snow, and the hair of His head like the pure wool: His throne was like the fiery flame, and His wheels as burning fire. A fiery stream issued and came forth from before Him: thousand thousands ministered unto Him, and ten thousand times ten thousand stood before Him: the judgment was set, and the books were opened.'

Daniel.

'For when the Gentiles, which have not the law, do by nature the things contained in the law, these having not the law, are a law unto themselves: which show the work of the law written in their hearts, their conscience also bearing witness, and their thoughts the meanwhile accusing or else excusing one another.'

Paul.

'But Abraham said, Son, remember that thou in thy lifetime receivedst thy good things, and likewise Lazarus evil things: but now he is comforted, and thou art tormented.'

The Lord.

I.
ANALOGY AND SCRIPTURE.

'The observation, that man is by his very nature a law to himself, pursued to its just consequences, is of the utmost importance; because from it will follow, that though men through stupidity or speculative scepticism be ignorant of, or disbelieve, any authority in the universe to punish the violation of this law; yet, if there should be such authority, they would be as really liable to punishment, as though they had been beforehand convinced that such punishment should follow.'—BISHOP BUTLER.

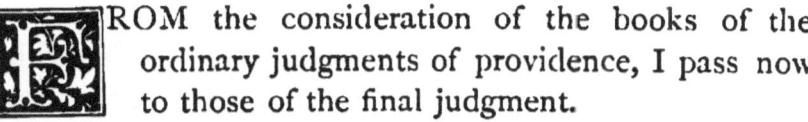ROM the consideration of the books of the ordinary judgments of providence, I pass now to those of the final judgment.

I assume that records of our lives are kept by God; and that these records, of whatever sort they be, can contain no facts which are not completely known to Him.

In order to a thorough and just judgment, however, which the final one is certain to be, it is necessary that the grounds of it—the facts on which it is to proceed—be known not only to the Judge, but also to those who are to be judged. In the twenty-fifth chapter of Matthew, indeed, we have conclusive information that it will be so; for when the righteous and the wicked, represented there in the Lord's own description of the judgment, severally plead ignorant, the one to the evil, the other to the good, ascribed to them by the Judge, He condescends to explain to them the meaning and effect of their bypast actions before He pronounces the awards. In other words, He lays bare to themselves the records on which He builds His judgments, that they as well as He may be convinced.

What are these records, or books, out of which the dead are to be judged? This is the question which must be handled first.

Looking abroad over the works of God, to discover from the arrangement and constitution of other things what we might expect in a divine judgment-book, we are met by this almost universal law, that every individual, living, and organized existence throughout the world contains within its own form the powers needful to develop it, and to enable it to fulfil those ends, which by the Creator it was intended to fulfil. Of which law we have this example, in the account of the third day's work in creation: 'God said, Let the earth bring forth grass, the herb yielding seed, and the fruit-tree yielding fruit after his kind, *whose seed is in itself*, upon the earth; and it was so. And the earth brought forth grass and herb yielding seed after his kind; and the tree yielding fruit, *whose seed was in itself*, after his kind: and God saw that it was good.' That is to say, the thing which appeared good to the Creator was, that the tree should not be obliged to an organism out of itself for its fruit, nor the grass for its seed; but that tree and grass should have *within themselves* their seed and fruit.

The same law is at work in the development of the human frame. It is by an organization within himself that the infant waxes into boyhood, and the boy again shoots up into the man. And when God's purpose with the man for this life is accomplished, that same organization which has hitherto built up his body, shall henceforth work to dissolve it and sink it into the grave.

When we pass out of the sphere of material creation into that of moral life, we are immediately impressed with the presence of a similar law. Man is appointed his own master, in so far as the choice of good or evil is concerned. To himself is committed the awful power of choosing or rejecting God. Man's own heart is the tablet on which God writes the expression of His will in conversion. The 'stony heart' is taken away, and a 'heart of flesh' bestowed, expressly for this end, that God may write upon the soft, new heart His holy law. And even to the man born and placed beyond the reach of a gospel which so changes the heart, there is still within himself a book of law, by which law, if he know no better, he shall be judged at last. We find, moreover, in the event of disobedience to this inner law, that the disobedient himself becomes the executioner of its vengeance. The instruments of punishment are concealed in his own being ; and without the necessity of external appliances, the flesh will wither from a bad man's bones, and cheerfulness of mind give place to horror and despair, by the judicial sentence of his own bosom alone.

Both in the region of the moral and material government of God, then, we find the law pervading, which appoints to each individual the working and administration of the judicial or provisionary concerns thereof, as the case may be. From the grass of the field, which has its seed in itself, to the mind of man which is the chamber-royal of human life, through every grade and form of intermediate existence, that law asserts its presence.

We seem, at the outset of our inquiry, therefore, entitled to expect, that there has been blended into the constitution of our own being, that which is symbolized by 'the books' of judgment. We find in ourselves the tablet on which God's law is written. We find the eye to read, and the will to choose, that law. We find, moreover, the instrumentalities which either reward or punish, according to the choice we make. It is only looking for a part of the actual whole we have already found, if we expect further to discover in ourselves, a recording faculty which shall preserve for final judgment some history of the deeds done in the body. Led by the analogies of divine arrangement in other things, we seem to have been brought fairly to the conclusion, that the judgment-book is some faculty of our own being; that, consequently, the opening of the books must be the quickening of that faculty in those who are judged; and now, under this first inquiry, it only remains for us to name what faculty of our being it is which may subserve this solemn end.

It must have suggested itself by this time to yourselves. There is one faculty we possess, and there is none besides, to which this peculiar work can be assigned. This faculty is our memory; the open and ever-opening record of our past thoughts and words and deeds: the book which is ever filling, and yet is never full,—in which every varying mood and fancy of the mind, every shape and vision of the imagination, every hope and fear, every joy and sorrow, every resolution we ever made, every covenant we ever broke, every relationship we ever entered, every duty we ever left undone, and all our acts of obedience and disobedience, of self-denial and indulgence, of virtue and vice,—are recorded with a faithful and unerring pen upon imperishable leaves. THIS, as I hope to show you, quickened in every man by the sight of man's Redeemer, shall be the record concerning which it is written : 'The dead were judged out of those things which were written in the books, according to their works.'

But to this conclusion, inasmuch as it relates to 'things which are unseen,' I should not be justified in leading you, unless the analogy on which it rests can be confirmed by Scripture. I have to ask now, therefore, whether Scripture countenances this interpretation of the books?

I have already referred to our Lord's account of the judgment, as illustrative of the fact, that man himself will bear a part in the production of the evidence on which he will be tried. I now turn to a very remarkable passage in the Epistle to the Romans, to confirm not so much the conclusion that memory particularly is the record, although by implication it does this also, as that it is some faculty in man himself. Paul had just given in the first chapter his comprehensive detail of the characteristics and progressive iniquity of heathenism ; and then, he suddenly turns round and confronts the reader of that detail, who, never thinking that it could apply to him, had assented to every word against the heathen, and joined in their condemnation : 'Therefore thou art inexcusable, O man, whosoever thou art that judgest; for wherein thou judgest another, thou condemnest thyself.' That is to say, the reader's own judgment of these poor heathen is proof, that within his own breast there lurks a knowledge, that such deeds as theirs are evil. But this very knowledge, this thing of the inner life, shall become, in the day of judgment, a ground of condemnation to himself, if he has been a doer of works like theirs. Accordingly, he is still further addressed in this startling language: 'After thy hardness and impenitent heart, thou (addressing one reader for all, and assuming their guilt) *treasurest up* unto thyself wrath against the day of wrath, and revelation of the righteous judgment of God.' In other words, the wrath which shall be poured out on that day is wrath taken from a treasury which the sinner is 'treasuring up unto himself,'—a form of expression, if not suggestive of, at least harmonizing with, the supposition, that it is some faculty in man himself which is the judgment-book. And it may be added, in precisely such language one would write who was thinking of memory as this faculty; for, as we shall immediately see, it is a treasury in whose heaped-up stores either wrath or blessedness may well be conceived as gathering against that day.

I shall quote, almost without comment, a few of the following verses, still further to confirm the general fact that the record, whether our memory or not, is a faculty within ourselves. The apostle is speaking of those who were without the law of Moses. I call your attention to the distinct manner in which he represents the whole judicial process as folded up in their own being.

There is a law; the power to obey it is implied; the witness of the obedience or disobedience is referred to; the accuser, the defender,—in short, the entire framework and instrumentalities of a prosecution and defence, —are included in the apostle's statement: 'When the Gentiles, who have not the law, do by nature the things contained in the law, these having not a law, are *a law unto themselves; which show the work of the law written in their hearts, their conscience also bearing witness, and their thoughts the meanwhile accusing or else excusing one another.*'

It is the prophet Malachi, however, who comes the nearest to an explicit statement that it is the memory specially which is the book of judgment. Speaking of those who feared the Lord, he says, 'They spake often one to another; and the Lord hearkened and heard it, and a *book of remembrance* was written before Him for them.' . . . Although it is stated of this book that it is 'written before God,' there is in this nothing inconsistent with the supposition that man's own remembrance is referred to.

In the seventy-seventh Psalm, there is a passing glimpse into the workings of memory which is worth referring to, in connection with this subject. The Psalmist says, 'I remembered God, and was troubled.' His trouble came to him through his memory. And as this trouble was a sense of condemnedness, there is at least a reflection of the probability, that the sense of condemnedness, which shall be wrought in the wicked at the day of judgment, may also enter through the memory.

But the most satisfactory testimony which we have, is borne in the parable of the rich man and Lazarus. The teaching of that parable carries us into the unseen world. The rich man in his palace, and Lazarus at the gate, are but the opening chapters in the story. The plot evolves and completes itself in the world beyond the grave. Every word of the conversation between Abraham and the rich man, therefore, must be replete with meaning. Listen to the following: The rich man being in torments, seeing Abraham afar off, and Lazarus in his bosom, cried, 'Father Abraham, have mercy on me, and send Lazarus, that he may dip the tip of his finger in water, and cool my tongue; for I am tormented in this flame.' But Abraham said, 'Son, remember that thou in thy lifetime receivedst thy good things, and Lazarus evil things: but now he is comforted, and thou art tormented.' SON, REMEMBER! At the very outset, an appeal to memory! Before he announced the reason why it was impossible for his request to be granted, the leaves of the sufferer's own recollection are referred to, and he is bidden read the grounds of the refusal there.

We had gathered previously by analogy, that it is not an unlikely thing that the record shall be some faculty within ourselves. We have now gathered out of Scripture confirmation of this fact, and indication besides, that memory is the particular faculty which God has appointed to be the record of our lives for the judgment-day.

II.

THE RECORDING ANGEL.

'The great Keeper, or Master of the Rolls of the soul, a power that can make amends for the speed of time, in causing him to leave behind him those things which else he would so carry away as if they had not been.'—Bishop Hall.

COME now to the very necessary consideration of the *fitness* of this particular faculty for the large and grave purposes of a judgment-book. If there be no fitness in it for such purposes, it is plain, the proofs I have submitted must go for nothing. We have simply mistaken their import. But, on the other hand, if there be in it such a fitness, we have therein an additional testimony and confirmation of the view on which I am insisting.

Now a judgment-book, to fulfil the ends which it has to serve, must contain a full body of evidence, and so arranged as to be easily referred to,—a requirement which the memory, and no other faculty of our mind, fulfils. It has been described sometimes as a book on whose leaves are written the actions of every day; sometimes as a storehouse into whose chambers are conveyed the multitudinous and manifold experiences of our lives; sometimes as an ocean into whose capacious bosom jewels and relics and wrecks of ships are deposited, which divers are striving to bring to light again; and sometimes, and not the least appropriately, to a grave which is ever receiving and yet is never full, and every day is giving back to life portions of its contents. But throughout all these modes of conceiving and representing the faculty, the same leading characteristic required in a right judgment-book can be found. For whether you look at memory through its resemblance to a grave, or an ocean, or a storehouse, or a book; or, withdrawing your mind from all semblances, attempt to look into the spiritual thing itself, to which we have given the name of memory, you will find in it this fitness for recording, and preserving, the records of passing events and experiences, which is indispensable in a judgment-book.

Among the wonders which our being contains, this wonder of memory—this power of recording the present and bringing it back out of the past—stands pre-eminent and apart. Like a distinct spirit within our spirits, it sits with its spiritual scroll, beholding through our eyes, and drinking in through our ears, and touching by our hands, whatever we see, or hear, or feel, or say. It is the historian of our lives. You cannot meet a stranger upon the streets, nor utter a word in your remotest solitude, nor think a thought in your inmost heart, but lo! this Recording Angel has noted it down upon the tablets of your soul for ever. And in far lands, after long lapses of time, in circumstances similar and dissimilar, when you are not thinking of the particular face, or speech, or deed, or thought, you will often find it brought back before your minds, and the whole past which surrounded it laid bare. So much is this sometimes the case, that you may remember to-day a face, a house, a scene, which you have not thought upon for many years, and which, perhaps, you only once beheld. No matter how slight that first glance may have been, up from the mysterious depths of your soul, through folds of intervening experiences and memories, shall arise the most transitory sights ever brought within range of your vision. And as with sights, so with sounds, and tastes, and smells. Whatever enters by the doorways of sensation, memory marks, records, and, when called upon, reproduces.

In nothing is this reproducing faculty noted more than in our actions. Sometimes a single action which was done in the bustle and stir of many others, arises, isolated from its companions, and presents itself to our contemplations. At other times, the actions of an entire period reappear and pass in review before us; of which the best illustration I can give is old age recollecting the scenes and companionships of youth. Take any old man: how busy his memory is with the past! Every day brings back portions of his early life. But that we may more fully acquaint ourselves with this far-reaching faculty, let us trace the history of the man, and observe the workings of his memory in its last decade. Recall his boyhood to your view. What a glory crowns it! He lives on the earth as a born king. The trees of all gardens, the fish of all rivers, the scope of all market-places, he claims for his own. His heart rejoices in freedom. Mountain height, and prickly heather, and stretch of street, can place no obstacle between him and the end he pursues. He draws companions around him by unconscious affinities. He singles out one to be his especial friend. With him he roams, with him he plays; to him he confides the innocent joys and sorrows, the mischievous designs and achievements, of his little life. The boy has friendship, joy, freedom, pleasure, and all the other gladsome lights of youth. Follow him into his manhood. How almost entirely the man has turned his back upon the enjoyments of his youth! A cold pride dims his recognition of the past. He hardly notices his early playmates or his especial friend on the street. Another world is around him. He is yoked to the chariot-wheels of care and business. The well of living water from which he drank in his boyhood is sealed up. Another and another care, like dead weights, press upon its mouth. The man schemes and toils as if he never had been young. But follow him yet another onward stage. Follow him until the great world of care and toil which sucked him into its whirl has cast him forth again. Follow him until old age has separated him from the bustle of business, from the strength and vigour of manhood, from the anxieties and ambitions of life, and seated him in the soft arm-chair by 'the ingle-cheek.' How freshly now return to him the scenes of his far-sundered youth! The curtain which concealed them for a time is raised once more, and they pass in new colours before his mind. Dim to him in comparison are the events of yesterday! He lives back amid experiences half a century old. The well is once more uncovered! The youth waters sparkle up! The early friends come back. Joy to the old man now, if his first friendships and boyish pleasures were unstained with crime! Pleasant, as the reward of the righteous, is the memory of one, whose youth was filled with reverence, and truth, and uprightness. There he sits, on his familiar seat, and the Recording Angel unfolds his scroll; and the words, and deeds, and emotions of innocent years return and shed joy and gladness over his heart. But 'wo and alas!' for the old man whose memory recalls a boyhood sullied by sin and crime. For then, to the external pains and weakness of age, shall be superadded the pangs of a vain remorse. A judgment-book, the book of his own memory, is unfolded before him, and he cannot choose but read.[1]

But here, and from this very instance of old age recollecting the experiences of youth, it may occur to some, that it is not enough to show that one particular period

---

[1] Readers of Wordsworth will remember his beautiful poem on memory, in which he handles this very subject. I am almost ashamed, in the presence of the lines which follow, to leave my rude and early daubing where it is. In the poem, memory is represented as a power whose 'pencil'

> 'works
> Those spectres to dilate;
> That startle conscience, as she lurks
> Within her lonely seat.
>
> 'O that our lives, which flee so fast,
> In purity were such,
> That not an image of the past
> Should fear that pencil's touch!
>
> 'Retirement then might hourly look
> Upon a soothing scene;
> Age steal to his allotted nook,
> Contented and serene.'—
>
> *Works*, vol. v.:
> *Poems of Sentiment and Reflection.*

of our lives can be brought back again, nor that stray actions and words are liable to be recalled. Before the admirable adaptation of memory to the purposes of a judgment-book can be fully seen, it must be known, whether all its leaves can be at once and instantaneously unfolded; whether, in short, it is so constituted as to be able, on the judgment-day, to give up the entire mass of facts on which the judgment must proceed.

Now memory is so constituted. Its laws are known to us, and this is known to be within the compass of their power. It may be added, they are as fixed and certain as the laws of the heavenly bodies. The associative power of ideas is the fountain from which they flow. What the force of gravitation is to the disposition and movements of the heavenly bodies, that, this power of association is to the contents of memory. By this one subtle, far-shooting, many-tendrilled power, these contents are laid hold of, recalled, arranged, and displayed to view. Yourselves have noticed the operation of this power. Whatever is associated in our thoughts with an idea, an act, an event, has the power thereafter of bringing it to our remembrance. The sight of the grave, for example, where you buried your neighbour, recalls that neighbour to remembrance. The sound of an air which you heard years ago will bring back the name or the form of the singer. The sight of a church, of a particular seat, of a particular text in your Bible, will recall a sermon, the impression it made, and the occasion on which it was delivered. It is simply necessary to bring into contact with the mind which you wish to excite to remembrance, some sight, or sound, or word associated with the thing to be remembered, and the obedient memory brings it forth.

It comes close to my subject to add, that the most startling operations of this power are to be found in the experiences of guilt. What sent Peter forth to weep so bitterly at the crowing of the cock? It was the remembrance of his Master's words which that crowing recalled. What blanches so visibly the criminal's cheek when an actual witness of his crime ascends the box? It is not alone the dread of conviction. It is also the effect on his own mind which the mere presence of a witness works,—laying open to his consciousness again the circumstances and reality of a guilt which law is blindly trying to establish. And what mystic power is that, within the steaming circle of debauch, which chills so instantaneously the heart of that wretched toper, and makes his blood run cold? It is a single word flung forth in a passing song. But the word was one which his sainted mother had used in her dying counsels, when she warned him away from the drunkard's path. And why is it, when all the reapers are full of mirth among the bending grain, when the gleesome rivalry, or the good-humoured joke prevails, that this particular one is forced back upon painful thought and hidden sorrow? It is because the very field they are reaping was the scene of an action which has darkened the whole path of life. Not one of the other reapers can see what is passing in their companion's mind. But there, as in a too faithful judgment-book, brought back to remembrance by the field,—the deed, the partners, the circumstances; the temptation, so weak at first, so strong at last; the help which might have come, but did not, because it was not sought; the madness in which the sin was wrought; the timorous after-pangs, quivering inwards into an agony of remorse when all was ended and irrevocable,—are painfully but scrupulously reproduced.

One thing only is needed, therefore, to our apprehension of the fact, that memory can subserve the purposes of a judgment-book. That one thing is the knowledge of an associating link so universal as to be connected with, and attachable to, every responsible action of our lives. For there must be, in order to a fair judgment, an unfolding of the entire scroll of life. And in order to this, there needs to be a certain thing, a word, or idea, or person, associated in our minds with the performance of every moral act; which thing or person, the Judge shall use to bring back into our memories the facts on which the judgment shall proceed.

From the illustrations already given, the least conversant with such subjects should be able to understand, how particular actions or periods of life might be recalled. The associated circumstances or persons might be made to play such a part, that memory would straightway turn over its pages, and lay open the passage in which the particular period or deed was recorded. And thus, action after action might be brought to light. But the tediousness and complexity of such a process would ill assort with the simplicity which distinguishes God's other works. And, expecting in this process a like simplicity, I go on to inquire,—whether, in every moral and responsible act, there be not a certain unvarying association, which *one thing*, whatever it is, shall be sufficient to recall, at once, the entire moral history before the mind? Now there certainly is such a presence—a presence contemporaneous not merely with some, but with every moral act we perform. It is to the description and illustration of this I next proceed.

III.

THE FACE OF THE JUDGE.

'The chief distinction in the person of Christ consists in His showing His wounds, according to the passage in Rev. i. 7: "Behold, He cometh with clouds; and every eye shall see Him, and they also which pierced Him." For this purpose His side is usually left bare, and the two hands are equally raised, with their pierced palms turned each exactly alike to the spectator. In this was set forth the great theological idea,—never absent from the person of Christ as judge, whether in Greek or Latin, in early or modern art,—that the wounds conveyed the respective sentences to the assembled children of men, according as they had previously accepted or rejected these signs of the atonement: to this one, the savour of death unto death; to the others, of life unto life,—the outward aspect of the Judge being the same to each. This greatly contributed to give that grand abstract air which befits the embodiment of divine justice. There is something indescribably fine in this rigid, full-front figure, which looks neither to the right nor the left, shows no favour and no resentment, but operates as a natural law, either to the salvation or confusion of those who behold Him.'—LADY EASTLAKE, *History of our Lord in Art.*

WHAT unlocks the memory? To what force, within or without, has been assigned the function of bringing its contents to light on the day of judgment? Let us recall, and bear along with us, what I have already established. I have, I think upon fair grounds, established that the books, which are to be opened at the judgment, are the memories of the judged.

And I am now advancing into the further inquiry concerning the opening of these books. How shall they be opened? By what process? With what instrumentalities? On this new search we have ascertained, that the human memory can be unlocked at any time by the power of association; by the entrance, that is, into the presence of the mind, of anything which was associated with the mind, when the word or deed, which memory brings back, was first given into her keeping. And the inquiry on which we are now entered is, What thing, power, influence, or faculty of our beings it is, which is associated in our minds with every moral act we perform? And how shall that be reached, and brought into use, in the processes of the judgment-day?

The first branch of the question may be answered at once. The *conscience* is that power within us, which is associated with every fact in our moral history. And *the knowledge of God in the keeping of the conscience* is, in all probability, the associating link which shall be used to summon and display together the facts of that history.

I recall to your minds that verse of Paul's already quoted, in which the conscience of the judged Gentile is described as 'bearing witness.' You are all familiar with a statement, that the conscience is the 'voice' or 'word' of God within us. It would be more correct to say that it *has* the word. But it is on this ground of its having, or being, the word or voice of God, that it is lifted into the office of witness-bearing. It is described as witnessing against the Gentiles, not because they were disobedient to the Mosaic or Christian law which they knew not, but because they were disobedient to a knowledge of God within themselves. In every man there exists such a knowledge, and this knowledge is the peculiar property of the conscience. There may be much knowledge; there may be all the knowledge brought down to us by Christ; or there may be no more than the natural mind can grope out among the revealings of creation. The fact I am directing you to is, that there *is*, in the possession of conscience, a knowledge of God; and that conscience is, in consequence, and to the extent of this possession, the setter forth of the divine mind and will within us. This is that inward light, which reveals to us the evil in our inclinations. This is that inward shadow, which darkens on our evil deeds. The monitions of this prophet of God within us have been addressed to us all. We cannot do a single responsible action, in reference to which a representation of the divine mind, exactly harmonizing with our previous knowledge of that mind, shall not be set before us by our conscience. Be that knowledge great or small, it is, to the extent of it, our law of God. And this law our conscience has in charge. It is this which is God's 'word' within us. And it is this word which is associated with every moral act we do.

Now there is in First Corinthians a very remarkable exhibition of the fact, that this word, or representation of the conscience concerning God, can be so acted upon as not merely to bear conviction into a sinner's own heart, but also bring forth that conviction in a judgment manifest to others. It is in that chapter where the apostle cautions the Corinthians to use prudently this gift of tongues; for if an unbelieving stranger, he says, were coming into your meeting, how insane your proceedings would appear! On the other hand, when you are simply, and in intelligible language, preaching, your words lay hold upon the stranger and convince him, and lead him to confess his unworthiness before you all. 'If all prophesy, and there come in one that believeth not, or one unlearned, he is convinced of all, and judged of all; and thus are the secrets of the heart made manifest: and so, falling down on his face, he will worship God, and report that God is in you of a truth.'[1] *Thus are the secrets of the heart made manifest!* By the simple utterance of the truth! By the presentation, in the words of another, of that same testimony which his conscience has already been plying him with! By holding up in his hearing, but in fresh, new, fuller aspects, the truth in his conscience which he had been putting away from his mind! The man is convinced; is more than convinced. His conviction comes out to light. And he is judged.

We only require, therefore, to lift this mode of convincing sinners into the circumstances of the judgment-day; we only require to know of a representation of the divine mind which the Judge may use, as His word was used in those Corinthian meetings, as it has been used for the conviction of sinners in all churches since; and, without venturing into a single speculation beyond the limits of our knowledge, we may reverently conceive how the secrets of our lives shall be made manifest then.— Now a representation of the divine mind, answering to this requirement, and postponed to the judgment-day, the Bible has actually set before us.

Among the facts on which stress is laid in the inspired

[1] xiv. 24, 25.

foreshadowings of the judgment, none is more noticeable than the *visible appearing* of the Judge : ' Behold, He cometh with clouds ; and every eye shall see Him, and they also who pierced Him ; and all the kindreds of the earth shall wail because of Him.' The *sight* of Him whom they pierced, is given as the external cause of the wail which follows. Corresponding to this are those passages, which describe the *face of God*, as the immediate cause of the dismay and confusion among the wicked on that day. One example of this, but applied rather to a physical than a moral effect, we find in the verse which precedes the text : ' I saw a great white throne, and Him who sat upon it ; *from whose face* the earth and the heaven fled away, and there was no place found for them.' Another example, and one expressly to the point, occurs after the opening of the sixth seal, where the kings and captains, and rich men and mighty, and every bondman and freeman, hid themselves in the dens and in the rocks of the mountains, and said, ' Fall on us, and hide us from *the face of Him* that sitteth on the throne, and from the wrath of the Lamb; for the great day of His wrath is come, and who shall be able to stand ?'

It is therefore a revealed fact, in connection with the judgment, that *the appearing of the Judge*, what is more specially termed 'the face of Him who sitteth upon the throne,' shall bring with it this certain influence, shall exercise this distinct function, of dismaying the guilty. And it does not seem to be venturing beyond the probabilities of this fact to conclude, that this, *the revelation, or visible appearing, of the face of the Judge, is the instrument appointed to unlock the memories of the judged.* Nor is it inconsistent with the known laws of our mind to conceive, that this outshining of the visible brightness of the Judge, this first distinct glance of His countenance, deepening into the look of Him who searcheth the hearts, and trieth the reins of the children of men, shall carry with it such a compass of association, over all the past actions of our lives, as must recall to us in a moment, what, either of good or of evil, we have ever done.

This face, embodying so much, identified with the view of divine truth which conscience contains, acting by laws in operation at present, would (for anything we know to the contrary) suffice to bring back before the consciousness of each the whole facts of the bypast life. Let the Lord appear to any of us, at this moment, and in all probability the phenomena of the judgment-books would be displayed at once. Nothing is more certain than the fact that He will appear, and that every eye shall see Him. In the scriptures referring to the event, a connection the most intimate and vital, is implied between that appearing and the feelings of the judged.[1]

Recall for a moment that rich scripture which speaks of 'the glory of God' as being in 'the face of Christ.' The 'face of Christ' in that scripture means simply, what Christ displays of God in the gospel. And the 'gospel' is just a representation of the character of God. The 'face of Christ' in the gospel, therefore, is the exhibition or view of God's character, fitted to convince and convert men's souls. The 'face of Christ' on his throne of judgment, again, is another expression of the same character, but in

---

[1] 'Every eye shall see Him, and they also which pierced Him: and all kindreds of the earth shall wail because of Him.'—Rev. i. 7.

its aspect of simple justice. The one is its embodiment and representation to *the eye of faith;* the other, its embodiment and representation to *the eye of sense.* In the one it is a word; in the other, a person. But the essential, the influential thing in both, is the character of God. And just as the ministration of the *figurative* face, or character of God, in the gospel, can seize upon a man now, and lay bare to him at one glance his sin and his Saviour, so (may we not reasonably expect?) the appearing of the *actual* face, in the day of judgment, shall be irresistibly and universally effectual, in laying bare the secrets of those who are then to be judged.

Now I have previously shown, that this essential influence, this representation of the divine mind or character, we have continually with us in our conscience. The 'word' in our conscience is our spiritual image or idea of God. It is to the eye of faith (as I have just been explaining) what the expression of God's face turned upon a moral action would be to the eye of sense. I mean by that,—if a dubious action were presented to a man's choice, there would appear within his bosom a representation, true to the extent of his knowledge, of the face from before which the earth and the heavens are to flee away. And after he had made his choice, if it were conceivable that Christ should personally appear before him, he would see, in the smile or frown of His countenance, the reality which his conscience had represented before.

For I must insist upon this, as the foundation of my answer to our present inquiry, that the face of Him whose seat is 'the great white throne,' is that same face, only clothed in glorified humanity, which our conscience brings to bear upon us every day at present. That awful face, which the righteous shall that day salute, from which the guilty shall shrink away, is the same which the righteous at this hour are kissing in the gospel, and which the wicked are putting scornfully away. It is that very face of which, as manifested in providence, we read that 'His eyes are upon the righteous, and His ears are open to their cry;' but He 'is against all them that do evil, to remove their name out of the earth:' the same, but taken from the keeping of conscience, and appropriated to the person of the Judge; the same, but lifted from a condition in which it can be seen only by the inward eye, to one in which it can flash in, through every percipient organ of our being, as an outward, embodied, and personal presence.

And thus shall an associating link to all the past actions of man's life be found! In 'the face' of the Judge,—identified with our previous knowledge of the divine character, recognised through all its features as that same image of righteousness and truth in the keeping of our conscience,—shall be displayed the august Presence, ordained to open the pages of memory, and summon into light every action of our lives!

IV.

OPENING OF THE BOOKS.

> Opened book! all eyes engages,
>   Bearing record of all ages,
>   Blazoned on its burning pages.
>
> Whence the Judge strict doom is sealing
>   Every hidden thought revealing,
>   None escaping, none appealing.
>
> Who, that now His coming feareth,
>   Who shall stand when He appeareth,
>   When the righteous scarce He cleareth?
>
> King of majesty tremendous,
>   Who dost free salvation send us,
>   Font of pity, O befriend us!   —*Dies Iræ.*[1]

THE supposition which I have thus ventured, I trust reverently, to make, to account for the recollections of the judged on the day of judgment, is one, which does not necessarily imply any alteration, in the powers or conditions, either of body or mind. But, on the other hand, neither does it overlook or exclude such a possibility. It is submitted as an explanation, which would probably be a sufficient one, if no such alteration were to take place. But in the event of certain alterations, its worth as a supposition would be immensely enhanced. Now undoubtedly there will be alterations—enlargement and elevation—of all the powers

[1] Rev. W. B. Robertson of Irvine's translation.

of our being, on the day when the secrets of life are to be disclosed by the appearing of the Judge ; and the original suggestion—that which Coleridge offered, and from which my own is a mere offshoot—proceeds, and indeed depends on the fact, that a very great change will be wrought, especially on the bodily powers.

'It would require,' he says, 'only a different and apportioned organization, the body celestial instead of the body terrestrial, to bring before every human soul the collective experience of its whole past existence.'

With a wider application—an application, I mean, to other objects besides those of memory—Archbishop Whately works out the same conjecture in his Lectures on the Future State :[1]—

'It seems to me not improbable, that the change which shall take place in the body may be itself the appointed means for bringing about a change in the powers and tendencies of the mind. . . . It is quite possible, that our minds may at this moment actually possess faculties which have never been exercised, and of which we have no notion whatever; which have lain inactive, unperceived, and undeveloped, for want of such a structure of bodily organs as is necessary to call them forth and give play to them' (the powers of sight, for example, in a blind man). . . . 'I think it is not unlikely that these (faculties) would be called into action by a mere change in our bodily organs, and a new system of organs. And if this should take place in a future state, we should at once be enabled to perceive, merely by means of a bodily change, whole classes of objects as new to our minds as colours are to a blind-born man ; and as totally different from any we are now acquainted with, as colours are with sounds. And by some change of this kind in the *brain*, an equally great revolution may, for aught we can tell, be produced in our *thinking* faculties also,—those by which we are distinguished from brutes,—and an equal enlargement produced in our powers of reasoning and judging.'

[1] *Scripture Revelations of a Future State*, Lect. v.

Let the change referred to, in these two extracts, be now taken into account; add to the suggestion already offered, respecting the associative power of the Judge's face, upon the contents of memory, the indubitable fact, that, either by resurrection or immediate change, all the powers of the human mind will be intensified and enlarged at the coming of the Judge; and the immediate and complete reproduction of the remembered past, is still more fully and satisfactorily explained. Assume the body celestial, and the disclosures of memory follow as a very natural result. Assume the intensified powers of mind which that body will certainly bring into our being, and the instantaneous and unreserved display of the contents of memory would be a mere corollary from the fact. By the conjoint action of those two new elements,—by the visible appearance of the Judge before the new and fuller organs of our changed nature,—the hidden page on which our lives are written would certainly be laid bare. And on that dread day, memory will prove faithful to the laws of her working; and the untold story of our lives shall be declared. And actions, passions, thoughts, and aims shall take their places on the unerring record: the reminiscences of the righteous, beautiful as the dawn of spring; the reminiscences of the wicked, terrible as the approach of death;—these, like venomous serpents, uncoiling themselves out of the rubbish and weeds of ruined cities; those, like sun-edged clouds ascending from the gates of the morning. And memory shall give up her dead. And the long-forgotten and unconfessed iniquities shall arise. And the unremembered charities which sought no praise, shall be brought forth to light. And up from her profoundest depths shall ascend the prayers, the sacrifices, the sympathies of the righteous,—the impure thoughts, the idle words, the shameful deeds of the wicked; and all the seeds and fruits of deliberated actions; and all the experiences, and circumstances, and events, which fill out and compose the history of our lives. And they shall become manifest on that day to our consciousness, as the fire which is henceforth to consume us, or the light by which we are to be crowned. And by no further exertion of the divine power than that by which existing laws are upheld! By the simple operation of a law which is at work at present! By the associative power on human memories of the Judge's 'face!' By the gleaming in, through our new perceptive organs, of the great reality, whose representation to our faith in time was the savour of life unto life, or of death unto death,—the opening of the books shall begin!

I seem to see the mingled wave of perturbation and joy, which shall sweep over the faces of those who shall be alive, and 'shall be changed,' when the Judge descends. I can almost realize how, for all those startled multitudes, the past shall open up at His approach and draw them backward,—*these* unto its abysses, *those* into its pleasant fields. He comes! The unbelieving are at length roused from their life-long delusion. In the features of the approaching Judge, they discern that same countenance, which looked out upon them from the gospel, which was set before them as the form and embodiment of divine mercy, and to which they were invited, but in vain, to look that they might be saved. And while they gaze, there arises, upon the waves of memory, every opportunity of accepting that mercy, and every scornful rejection of its claims. He comes! The impure souls shrink from the awful light. That Eye, holy and severe, which gazed on them from the unseen, in their own knowledge of the truth, before all their deeds of vileness, and pled with them to resist, has searched them out. And in a moment, the loathsome scenes of their impurity, the circumstances and partners of their sin, are recalled and portrayed upon their souls with all the vividness of the actual past. He comes! The cloak of the wretched hypocrite is rent into pieces. There is that divine countenance which they could so eloquently depict, which yet they never loved; which they ever, ever, ever mocked with hollow and disloyal homage, to live among vain shows! He comes! And every eye shall see Him; and they who pierced Him shall mourn. And the dishonest, the slanderous, the unmerciful, all who opposed His cause, and all who resisted His truth, shall have to endure the glance of that consuming brightness. There is no concealment more. Embodied in glory, terrible in power, shines forth that very countenance of truth, and love, and goodness, which the wicked beheld with averted eyes, and blasphemed and scorned, when it looked, from the gospel message, beseechingly upon their miserable souls! And even as they gaze, the associative power of that countenance upon their memories shall have cleft the wall which divided them from the past, and thrust them back into the horrid forms and circumstances of their ungodly lives, to read the reasons of their condemnation there.¹

But, on the other hand, on that dread day, with what an irridescence of joy the same sight shall strike down into the palpitating consciousness of the redeemed! In them shall be mental resurrections of pleasant sights and scenes. The widow shall see her mite once more. The cup of cold water given in Christ's name shall not fail to reappear. Homes which were the abodes of virtue, shall rise mysteriously from the depths of memory; and hospitals, whose floors were trodden by the visitants of the sick. And memory shall go feeling-down for churches, whose walls have long since crumbled into dust. And the swell of public prayer and praise shall renew their emotions in many a soul. And blessed thoughts, and deeds, and lives shall be remembered. But, above all, and more blessed than all, and in every saint, there shall arise the remembrance of Jesus,—of His love, of His mercy, of His help,—as the seed and cause of all other remembered good. And memory shall find her sweetest

---

[1] 'He saw at last into the awful reality of things: religion—the phantom of this world—substantiated in all its terrific truth, and the solid-seeming world the phantom in its stead. The ghastly reality, so long evaded, would be put by no longer. Conscience was to sleep no more. The vastness of the loss, the hopelessness of the doom, the infatuation of the delusion, all burst upon him. His heart withered within, and "he was speechless." But through all the horrible silence of the time, while all heaven was mute to hear, his ear could catch the awful voice that spoke, never to be again heard, but to leave its dread echo for all eternity within the heart: "Bind him hand and foot, and take him away, and cast him into outer darkness; there shall be wailing and gnashing of teeth."'— ARCHER BUTLER: *Sermon on the Wedding Garment.*

triumphs in the reproduction of the treasures laid up in heaven.

Of one thing we may well be sure, that the approach of the Judge to the righteous, will be the reappearing of that spiritual form in their sanctified conscience, whose countenance darkened as they drew near to evil, and glowed with approving love when they accomplished good. The very smile, methinks, which shall lighten up His face, as He utters the words, 'Well done, good and faithful servant,' shall be identified with the joyous aspect which the conscience turned upon the soul when besetting sins were overcome.

Thus, as I humbly conceive it, shall the books be opened! At the first glance of the Judge's face! The whole may be the work of a moment. A moment may serve to light up the hieroglyphic transparencies of the soul. Then, perhaps for the first time, we may fully realize how fearfully and wonderfully we are made; and of our memory alone have to be taught, how deep and far-reaching is her capacity and strength. Then, when the face of the Eternal shall bid her forth, and she has to come up from her dwelling-place in the soul, like some weird angel of the wilderness, carrying in her loaded arms, the proofs and documents on which our trials shall proceed. No tedious process shall be required to force the truth into light. No separate and outward book needs to be produced. Our own memory is the book; and the face of God shall open it.

Consider this, all ye who are living in secret sin! Consider this, ye who steal out in the darkness to do deeds of shame! Consider this, ye who are cherishing ungodly thoughts, and following ungodly aims! You may not seem to others the guilty spirits which you are. But not the less you are ripening for the righteous judgment to come. A recorder in your own souls is even now recording your doings truly. A judge in your own bosoms is even now judging your actions justly. And the day is coming when that same judge shall appear in terrible majesty, and search that record of your lives, and bring every hidden thing to light. And if you had buried your wickedness in the very shadow of death, the brightness of His face would display it like the day.

One other remark. It can hardly fail to have been noticed how my illustration ever tended to take its instances from the side of guilt. I have now to explain that it was not accidental that it did so. It is only incidentally that the righteous are concerned with 'the books' of judgment. 'Another book' is to be opened, 'the Book of Life;' and this is pre-eminently the book of the righteous. I reserve the explanation of that other book to the chapters which follow. But lest there be any soul, tender to the concerns of its eternal well-being, who may have been disturbed from the peace of the assurance which flows from the blood of Christ, by the predominant tendency of my illustration,—any truly saved soul who may have been driven back upon itself, upon its memory of many sins,—I shall quote for such an one this blessed and reassuring word: 'Son, daughter, be of good cheer; *thy* sins are forgiven thee.' Although the ground of the sinner's condemnation is to be sought in himself, and the record of it in his memory, the ground of the saint's justification is to be found in God. Be not afraid, thou beloved one. 'There is therefore now no condemnation to them who are in Christ Jesus.' Abide in Him. Pray that your name be not blotted out from that other book. Pray and strive to be kept within the blessedness of the life 'whose sin is covered, unto whom the Lord imputeth not iniquity, and in whose spirit there is no guile.'

> Almighty Judge, how shall poor wretches brook
>   Thy dreadful look,
> Able a heart of iron to appal,
>   When Thou shalt call
> For every man's peculiar book?
>
> What others mean to do, I know not well;
>   Yet I hear tell
> That some will turn Thee to some leaves therein
>   So void of sin,
> That they in merit shall excel.
>
> But I resolve, when Thou shalt call for mine,
>   That to decline,
> And thrust a testament into Thy hand!
>   Let *that* be scanned:
> There Thou shalt find my faults are Thine.

GEORGE HERBERT.

Part Fifth.

THE BOOK OF LIFE;

OR,

BOOK OF THE NAMES, MANIFESTATION AND DESTINY OF THE SONS OF GOD.

'And another book was opened, which is the book of life.'

'And whosoever was not found written in the book of life was cast into the lake of fire.'

John.

'In this rejoice not, that the spirits are subject unto you; but rather rejoice because your names are written in heaven.'

'He that overcometh, the same shall be clothed in white raiment; and I will not blot out his name out of the book of life, but I will confess his name before my Father and before His angels.'

'And I will write upon him the name of my God, and the name of the city of my God, and my new name.'

The Lord.

'We all, with open face beholding as in a glass the glory of the Lord, are changed into the same image from glory to glory, even as by the Spirit of the Lord.'

'Those women who laboured with me in the gospel, with Clement also, and with other my fellow-labourers, whose names are in the book of life.'

'That in the ages to come, He might show the exceeding riches of His grace, in His kindness toward us through Jesus Christ.'

Paul.

'Which things the angels desire to look into.'

Peter.

I.

A FAMILY REGISTER.

'The first-born—written in heaven.'

BETWEEN the 'books' of the final judgment already considered, and this other, 'the book of life,' whatever further differences we may find, this strikes us at the threshold, that whereas the former represent innumerable separate and individual records, viz. the memories of the judged; this one is the symbol of some large and simple unity: these are the 'books'—this, the 'book.'

And this also we may see while still upon the threshold, that it is the book, not merely as distinguishing it from preceding books, but by this pre-eminence, that the awards to the righteous and the wicked are ultimately made upon its showing alone. For they who are to be cast into the lake of fire are simply they who shall *not* be found in the book; and in like manner, only they are to enter the holy city who *are* written therein.

Of the otherwise high place among the instruments of the divine government which this book occupies, we may form some idea by considering the occasions besides the present on which mention is made of it. Twice in this same portion of scripture, the dwellers on the earth who were to secede to the worship of the beast, are characterized by this single stroke, that their names are not written in the book.[1] Once, in the epistle to the church of Sardis, it is held up as an inducement to repentance, that the overcomer's name would not be blotted out.[2] And in the Epistle to the Philippians, Paul, speaking of his fellow-labourers in the gospel, exhausts all praise of them by this brief addition: 'whose names are in the book of life.'[3] Moses, when interceding with God, on the occasion of the calf-worship, for the pardon of the Israelites, reserved this touching request to the last: 'Forgive my people, O Lord; and if not'—he could find no alternative that would express a deeper sincerity and sorrow—'if not, blot me out of the book which thou hast written.'[4] And in the sixty-ninth Psalm, the Psalmist, speaking as the man of God oppressed by the earth, winds up his prayer for vengeance with this stern wish: 'Let them be blotted out of the book of the living, and not be written with the righteous.'[5] And finally, to be 'written with the righteous,' the Lord taught His disciples, was to be looked upon as a ground of rejoicing, deeper and surer than even the ability to cast out devils. 'In this rejoice not, that the spirits are subject to you, but rather rejoice because your names are written in heaven.'[6]

To the study of this other book, then, to be written in which is our highest gain, to be blotted out of which our profoundest loss, I proceed now.

The elementary basis of the symbol, that out of which its form of a book has arisen, is very obviously the record of children's names usually kept by families. This ele-

---

[1] Rev. xiii. 8, xvii. 8.   [2] Rev. iii. 5.   [3] Phil. iv. 3.
[4] Ex. xxxii. 32.   [5] Ps. lxix. 28.   [6] Luke x. 20.

ment crops out in the description which we find in the Epistle to the Hebrews, of the general assembly and church into which Christians come. It is 'the church of the first-born, written in heaven;' in other words, the church of the children named in God's book. In God's family each child is looked upon and treated as a first-born. The book of life is the register of their names. This, at least, is its simplest and most primitive feature, and the one with which at the outset we require to acquaint ourselves. Whatever clearer light we may obtain, in the progress of our inquiry, as to its substance and character, the thing on which that light must fall will continue to be a family roll.

By giving prominence thus early to this first feature of the book, I would not be understood as shutting out that later and larger feature, which seems to have been chiefly present to the minds of Paul and John, whereby it would fall to be described rather as a register of citizens. For it is a register of citizens also. It is at the coming down of 'that great city, the holy Jerusalem, out of heaven,' that its final testimony is appealed to for the names of those who are to enter in. Only, this is not the basis of the symbol; and it is the basis or fundamental element we are asking about at present. I find *that* in the family record alone. I know, indeed, that in the progress of God's kingdom, the family-life is drawn up into the city-life: that the child-tie develops into the citizen-tie; that the household of faith is built out into the kingdom. But the elementary band remains. It is a kingdom of children still. Its citizenship begins and ends in sonship. And when the roll of the city shall be completed, this deeper fact will appear written over against all its names, that they are first of all the children of the city's King.

I shall therefore, for the present, keep by the simpler and more primitive type. I shall take the family record as our best idea to begin with of the record in heaven. Of such records, traced from current generations back to Adam, the Bible, as you know, is full. But, as lying nearer to ourselves, and because substantially it is the same kind of record which these Scripture genealogies are, I shall rather specify—to give you an idea of the elementary form of the book of life—the list of names so familiar to us in the blank leaves of our family Bibles. What that list is to our homesteads here, the book of life essentially is to our home in heaven. In both cases there is a family roll; and in both cases it is a roll filled in by a paternal hand. Except that the one embraces usually but the lives of two generations, and the other all the generations of the great family of God; except, further, that the blotting out from the domestic record is in consequence of bodily death, and from the heavenly record in consequence of spiritual death, there is a close and natural similarity between the two. A similar yearning for objects of love has brooded over the empty page of each. In each the names have been entered with joy and rejoicing; and each, in its own way, could show where the tear was dropped, when a name once entered had to be blotted out. At the top, in our family Bibles, are the reverend names of father and mother; beneath them, like a stately pillar, the names of their offspring. Here the first-born was entered; and, next to him, the boy who went to sea; and this is Dora's name; and this is little Willie's, blotted out by death; and other names to the close. Even such a register, in the simplest conception of it, is the book of life: the Father's name—the 'God-begat'—at the top, with entries and blottings out the same. Here was Cain's place, and here Esau's, and here the blank which Judas filled. There, like a drawn sword, is the name of him whom the Lord would not blot out—Moses, the man of God. There, burning like the morning star, is the great name of father Abraham. Ezekiel's is farther down, and between are David's, and Elijah's, and Isaiah's. High on the forehead of the goodly register beam the names of the world's first teachers, Adam and Enoch, and the builder of the ark. In that little cluster are the names of the prophets; in that below, the names of the disciples. And here, stretching down to our own day, is the long roll of those who sealed their faith with their blood: Abel and the martyred prophets, Stephen and Paul, Antipas and Huss, Patrick Hamilton and Cargill, and South-Sea Williams. Here are the scholars who consecrated their scholarship to God; here the great preachers who proclaimed His word. And up and down, through all the list, are beaded-in the immortal names of the daughters of God. I read Miriam's and Deborah's, and the names of Sarah, and Ruth, and Naomi. Mary's is resplendent as the moon; and beside it shine the names of the other Mary and Mary Magdalene. And Martha's is not blotted out. And lower, but not in dignity, are the names of Dorcas, and Phebe, and Lydia, and Priscilla. And the names of those dear souls who have gone from our own circles and in our own day. And myriads more. Names of which the world took no note are noted here. No true name is forgotten. Even the penitent thief has a place; and all besides who turned from sin to God; and all who have lived to God, and all who have died to God: Job, and with him every faithful steward of wealth; Lazarus, and with him every faithful endurer of poverty; and Greek and barbarian, and bond and free. And, intermingled in the blessed catalogue, the hidden names of those who were hardly named on earth, who could not discern between their right hand and their left, who put forth a mere promise of buds below, and were taken to bloom above.

II.

THE NAMES IN THE BOOK.

> 'Those that within the house of God
>   Are planted by His grace,
> They shall grow up, and flourish all
>   In our God's holy place.
>
> 'And in old age, when others fade,
>   They fruit still forth shall bring;
> They shall be fat and full of sap,
>   And aye be flourishing.'

SO much regarding the book of life it was allowable to set forth in the terms of our simplest conception. And this much, gathered though it has been while standing on the outmost edge of the mystery, it is necessary to carry along with us. The book of life is a family register. The names which it contains are the names of God's children. But now I advance our inquiry another step, and indicate my second position by the statement that *the names*, with which we have been refreshing our memories, *are themselves a portion of the symbol*—the thing to be explained; and are consequently not to be received as the literal names inscribed in the book of life.

The names of Martha and Mary, of David and Job, and of all the saints I have referred to, are indeed in-

scribed. Their actual *names* are. But 'Mary' and
'Martha,' and 'David' and 'Job,' are not these names.
I have some right to suppose that Mary's name in the
heavenly record is, ' seeker of the one thing needful;' and
Martha's, 'carer about many things;' and David's, ' the
man according to God's own heart;' and Job's, 'the man
perfect and upright, who feared God and eschewed evil.'
It would not be a correct book otherwise. The family
names of earth are accidents, memorials of ancestors,
tributes of affection to living relatives, echoes and copies
of names made common by rank or history, things affixed
to the outside of us, meaningless, not intended to have
meaning, without the remotest reference to the inner life of
those who are to answer to them. In the divine register
these fond but inexpressive names can have no place. A
man's name there is the expression of what a man is.
The Shepherd 'knoweth his own,' and by what He knows
of them they are called. Of one He knows that he is
' poor in spirit;' of another, that he is a 'peacemaker;'
of a third, that 'he hungers and thirsts after righteousness.' One is 'faithful;' a second is 'hopeful;' a third
' forgives as he was forgiven.' Some have names taken
from their filling well some sphere of private life; others
from their faithful filling of an exalted sphere. And by
these names He calleth them. ' He calleth His own
sheep by name.' No one has an unmeaning or accidental
name with Christ. The name is grounded on the character, or inner peculiarity of life. And this peculiarity,
exactly expressed, is the name entered on the book of life.

Glimpses of this, taking place even here, are afforded
both in the Old Testament and the New. New names

corresponding either to their position, life, purpose, character, or gift, are bestowed by God upon His servants. The first woman, in her penitence, becomes 'Eve,' or life. Abram becomes 'Abraham,' the father of nations. Jacob becomes 'Israel,' or wrestler with God. Our Lord gives new names to His apostles. To Simon, who first among them all confesses Him, who is also to take the lead in building up His kingdom, He gives the name of 'Peter,' or stone, among all the living stones of the new temple, the first to find its place on the foundation, and therefore the stone on which all that follow must successively be laid. But to Saul, who was to become His messenger to the Gentiles, His toiling, unwearying servant, the man of labours manifold, the preacher of the cross, and builder up of the Church, is given the not less honourable name of Paul, or worker.

Besides these glimpses, we have conclusive proof of what I have advanced, in the promise to give new names to those who overcome. And perhaps, the common practice of naming children at their baptism, of giving what we call the Christian name,—although it is, as we have seen, the giving of names which have no connection with the inner life,—not only may indicate the recognition by the Church of the sacredness of names, but also instinctively typify the truer ultimate naming of heaven. Of this there can be no doubt:—whatever other mystery may be intended by baptism, to baptize a child into the Name of the Three-one God, is to consecrate that child to a life which shall be an image or reproduction of that Name.

Take this along with you, then, as our second fact,

that a man's name in the book of life is not the Robert, or William, or John, by which he is known among men, but that true, divinely applied word, which expresses the character he sustains before God.

And this leads me to take up my third position, which is, that *character*—the fact expressed by the 'Name' in the book of life — *is just another expression for the amount and form of spiritual life we have.* The estimate formed of us by people around us, is not our character. Our character is the peculiar form of our spiritual life. Essentially it is that, and only that. Straight or crooked; large or little; stunted or well-developed,—the actual, realized, inner form of life is the character, and nothing else is. High standing in the eyes of the world, or the Church, counts for nothing. Large life is written down 'large life;' little life is written down 'little life.' And if there be *no* life—nothing of Christ within—there is no character. It is a nameless soul; a dead, uncounted soul. It is not named in the book.

And by this fact, we pass upward into the true conception and real nature of this celestial roll. It is the book of *life*. Life is its special and essential secret. And the one ultimate purpose of all life—life of matter as much as life of soul—is to produce name, or character. I go out on a spring day to the woods. The ash and the beech are putting forth their leaves. The grass is freshening beneath my feet. The swallows are looking for their old nooks in the windows. The lambs are bleating on the hill. From the central depths of the earth, life is rushing and steaming upwards—seeking books on which to write its names. I read in the book of birds: not two swallows are alike; not two feathers of the same swallow. I read in the book of trees: the elm differs from the oak; the leaves of the oak from one another. I take up two blades of grass; they differ. Difference, character, name. meet me on the minutest leaf and atom of matter. I observe the growth of a little child. She came soft and round into our keeping, neither like nor unlike those who came before. But her growth is the growth of character. Life blocks her out into her peculiar shape. Life writes out its form—its name—on face and hands and feet, on words and looks and deeds. It is the law of life. All life hastens to express its word, or name. Vegetable and animal life have their respective handwriting, their methods of inscribing, registering, and naming the subjects in their kingdom. In the complex natural life of man, the same law prevails. Would it not be strange if spiritual life were without it? For what is this higher life, this life of life, this life of the soul? Nothing less than the reception into the heart of God's own life. But it is the reception of this life, if I might so explain it, molten and poured out for us into a Name. And this name is Christ. He is pre-eminently *the* name of God—the Word, the express image of His person. Receiving Him into the heart, we receive the formative principle of all true character, the very image and name of God; and therein an influence, that will go on moulding, shaping, forming us, until the entire personality, the whole human life within us, has attained to some measure of likeness, to some namely accordance and harmony with His own.

'I am the Vine, ye are the branches.' The whole mystery is contained in these words. It is the divine life of Christ entering into and pervading a man, and causing him to bloom and put forth fruit, as the sap of the tree does to its branches. And just as the shock of life in that tree shoots and penetrates to the remotest twig, just as the processes of budding and leafing and fructifying are certain results of the vital power at the centre, so does the life of Christ,—the vital power, the character-giving principle in the heart of a believer,—propagate direct from the heart of God, through all the channels of our being, His thoughts, His feelings, His ways; in other words, what we are appointed to receive of His name or character.

Christ's life cannot be in the heart without leading to this result. The hand that knocks at the door, knocks that it may come in and write upon the walls. His name is announced in the word, that we may feel our connection with it, and realize something of that name for ourselves. He says 'God,' that we may answer 'godly.' He says 'Christ,' that we may be formed into christians. He says 'Lamb,' that we may at once know of His atoning death, of the forgiveness which is in His blood, and of the life of sacrifice to which He is calling us. But always, in every utterance of His name, it is His purpose to beget and develop within us, form, character, or name, like His own.

And thus we reach and touch the very secret of this book of life. Where the divine purpose in Christ, which I have just referred to, is realized, and character is formed, there is,—in the very attainment of that,—a realization of what is symbolized by the words, 'written in the book of life.' And where this purpose is not being realized,—where there is no formation of character, no rising to higher measures and purer developments of life, there is the absence of this reality,—there is no such in-writing. For what we here describe, as the handwriting of Christ in the book of life, is, when the fact is disengaged from its symbol, simply the formation of Christian character in the soul. A character fairly formed, a something of Christ's image attained to,—that is our name, our coming up out of chaos, out of the void, out of darkness; it is our putting forth of leaves and fruit, our registration in the book of life. And on the other hand, the loss of this character,—of the meekness, and gentleness, and love, and faith, and hope which composed it,—that (supposing it to occur) would be the blotting out of our names. Life is suspended in such a case. We have let go the formative principle. We have put out of all our thoughts the name of the Lamb, the truth or word, which God has given to shape us into heavenly beauty. And just as the dead leaf loses, first its elasticity, then its colour, then its shape; just as bodily death blots out the light of the eyes, and the bloom of the cheek, and the roundness of the form, and one by one takes away every mark and feature of personality, until only a handful of dust is left,—so is the departure of Christ's life from the soul of man, accompanied and followed by the breaking down and withdrawal of all the marks and images of heavenly things which it impressed; and we return into chaos, into the region of formlessness, and our place is darkened out of the book of life. There may still be present in our earthly life, pursuits, ambitions, joys, sorrows, all the activities of worldly men. The man, by his achievements in thought or action, may be carving out for himself a name in the memory and esteem of his generation; but true life is gone. The testimony of the Bible regarding him is that he is 'dead.' He is a dead soul. Death is the inner fact—the destroying force—in his being. From the hour that he put away from him the life of the Lamb of God, and separated himself to do his own will, to live in his own strength, and to please himself, he has been dead. The processes of spiritual death are advancing without and within. The image of Christ—what of the divine character he had attained to—is being ground down and scattered. His name has been growing dim, and ever dimmer, on the page of the book of life. He has no longer a shape and a character in the sight of God. He has ceased to be 'written in heaven.' On earth 'he has a name to live;' but he is 'dead.' He is no longer among those whom the Shepherd 'knoweth, and calleth by name.' At last, it has to be said of him, that he has ceased to be 'written among the living.' In 'that day,' he will not be found written in the book of life.

III.

FORMATION OF CHARACTER.

'It is not in words explicable with what divine lines and lights the exercise of godliness and charity will mould and gild the hardest and coldest countenance, neither to what darkness their departure will consign even the loveliest. For there is not any virtue the exercise of which, even momentarily, will not impress a new fairness upon the features; neither on them only, but on the whole body.'—RUSKIN.

NLESS I have conveyed my meaning darkly, I have now submitted explanations of the *form*, *contents*, and *vital character* of the book.

In form it is *a book*, because essentially it is the roll or register of the divine family; the '*names*' which it contains are the peculiar shapes, the individualities of character, which distinguish one from another in that family; and it is a book *of life*, because these names or inner forms of character, are the issue and result of actual life, of that divine life by which souls become living souls.

I trust I have now done enough, to prepare the way for my fourth position, which is, that *this name or character*,—this form of the inner life, working from within outwards,—*at length impresses itself on the very body*.

Is it venturing too far, to attempt to embody some faint conception of the manner, in which this impressment is made, and the names of the soul expressed, in their full significance, in the forms of the bodily life? I remember how circumscribed the ground is, in relation to such processes, which revelation has laid bare; but looking around and within, I seem to find, in the sphere of our daily observation, facts which only need to be struck to emit light on this process.

And first of all,—and as a necessary background in the illustration of this impressment of names,—there is that law, with which we have already become so familiar in our study of the book sealed with seals—the law by which evil inscribes its autographs and Cain-marks on the life of the evil-doer. You can easily recall illustrations of that law. You have seen, crossing your path on the highway, or flitting past you in the crowd, beings so abject and full of misery, so bloated and unsightly, as to have flashed into your minds a momentary doubt, whether they were human beings at all. Almost the form of humanity was gone. There was a crouching and a dimness upon the moving mass. For the erect and comely elasticity of the human frame, there was the ungainly and angular movements of worms and certain beasts of burden. The light of the countenance was quenched. The eyes were sunk. The lips had lost their curves of decision, and an impression of brutishness came out upon you from every other feature. You know the secret of such phenomena. You do not hesitate to account for the debasement of the outer form, by a foregoing debasement of the form within. First, the character of the soul broke down, and then the character of the body. First, the man separated himself from that life which, if he had retained, would have put forth the beautiful features, the strength and style of a higher being; then, the absence of that inner life was followed by the destroying forces of inner death; then, the moral scaffolding being rotted away, the unsanctified body, like an uncompleted arch, descended into lower and more hopeless ruin.

In the majority of cases, indeed, this debasement of the outer form, under the influence of evil, does not reveal itself to the common eye. Preservative influences from without, food, clothing, polished society, gymnastics, may do much to keep the lustre in the eye, and the radiance upon the cheek. But it is only an appearance. Beneath the outward polish and unbedimmed exterior, there is vital bedimment, debasement, mouldering away. It was of such the Lord was speaking when He said: 'Give not that which is holy unto the dogs, neither cast ye your pearls before swine.' It was human dogs, human swine He meant.[1] The form of the spirit regulates that of the body. The dog-spirit has the dog-body. The swine-spirit has the swine-body. The inner name, or character writes its corresponding name, or character without.

But now, in the next place, and over against these facts, I have to state that this law does not manifest itself in debasing influences alone. Ever, above or below, spirit presses into form, into outer and visible form. The walk of the sluggard is literally, as some anatomists have defined

---

[1] 'If we are to find here two different characters of bestial opposers, we should rather say that the "dogs" were the unclean, the utterly and shamelessly sunken in impure lusts (Rev. xxii. 15); the "swine," the fierce and bitter opponents of the truth of God (comp. Ps. lxxx. 13: "The wild boar out of the wood doth root it out"): the first, the Heliogabalus; the second, the Galerius.'—TRENCH: *Serm. Mt.* in loc.

all walking, 'a falling forward;' that of the industrious man is a tread. The brow of the man of thought has thought written upon it; a brow of equal size on a man who lets his mind lie waste, looks little and inexpressive. Industry, thought, every fact of the formed soul within, writes a corresponding fact upon the formed body without. How often, in the performance of some heroic action,—in lifting a drowning child, for instance, above the waves, or in making protest in the face of tyranny against some great iniquity,—has the tiniest form seemed to swell up into vast dimensions! The frame dilates, the eye kindles, the breast heaves, the whole bearing puts on nobleness. Even a crowd gathered out of the streets rises into a higher shape under the influence of one noble word. The separate atoms coalesce, a band of living fire shoots from brain to brain, the mass heaves to and fro with the impulses of a common excitement, arms are lifted into the air as if they were the arms of a single being, and ten thousand voices rush into one, like a peal of thunder in the sky.

And it is not in accidental flashes, in momentary outbreaks alone, that this formative influence is developed. It is a characteristic, continuous, steady fact of our moral nature.

Did you ever notice the countenance of an intelligent boy when some truth—even a mere truth concerning the material world—was for the first time announced to him? His whole face took on a glow of delight. If you habituate a mind like his to the incursion of new truth, that glow will become, to a certain extent, the habit of his countenance. We cannot take a new truth into our mind, or act in the power of it for any time, but it seeks to express itself in some way upon our being. The higher the truth is, the greater is the influence! Let the truth received and acted out be the gospel—the sum of all truth, the revelation of the very and perfect image of God. From the moment this is admitted into the soul, it begins to act upon us, and shape us, and change us into the very image it reveals. Our face shines with a new beauty; our very bearing assumes something of the port of heaven. Look at any young man who has been living, for some years, to the Lord! What has written manliness, gentleness, and purity, on every page of his life? It is the truth of manliness, gentleness, and purity, which he received in the principles and spirit of the gospel. This result, of course, cannot in all cases be a visible one. In this, as in other things, there will often be the working of a life, which is still hid with God. But the process, none the less, is always going on; and such foregleams and outflashings of it occur, that even the eyes of the most debased will at times discover in it a glory, which is not common to our race. No one who has read Mrs Fry's life can forget that passage, in which her first visit to the female prisoners in Newgate is recorded. She ventured alone, into a large room, occupied by the worst outcasts of her sex. Sin and crime had trampled out their womanly looks and beauty. They received the dressed lady with grins and laughter, with scowling eyes and rude words. But she took out her Bible and began to read. First one, then a second, then a third came round to where she sat. The mad laughter and rudeness subsided. The gibes and the fury sunk silent. And, one by one, they all drew near, and the reading of the passage was finished amid the hushed attention of the rudest there. When at length, she stepped towards the door to leave, one of the women darted forward to open it for her. And when the lady, touched by this little service, said, 'I thank you,' the poor prisoner hushed down her thanks, and, as if her better nature had risen for the moment from the deep, replied, 'No thanks, my lady, *the angels have lent their voices to you.*' Dark though the soul of this fallen one may have become by sin, she could yet see and hear, in this visitor of her prison, the beauty and music of a heavenly world.

Ever it is so. The life which by Christ's grace is daily growing more beautiful within, will daily put forth more beauty to the surface. It fascinates us by its depths of unpretending worth. The beautiful temper sheds its dawn through every feature of the body. A something beams out through the countenance, and takes you prisoner by its loveliness. The clay yields to the informing spirit. The plainest features receive a glory from within. And when skin-deep beauty has lost all its radiance, this, even in old age, has still

> 'Smiles to earth unknown ;
> Smiles, that with motion of their own
> Do spread, and sink, and rise ;
> That come and go with endless play,
> And ever as they pass away,
> Are hidden in her eyes.'[1]

But I need not dwell on such illustrations.[2] I shall

---

[1] Wordsworth's *Louisa*.

[2] And yet, I must not forbear repeating here, some sentences from the closing chapter of a story, which a friend has well told, about a

lead you to the greatest which can be appealed to. One, and not the lowest, purpose of the transfiguration of our Lord, was to bear witness to this very law. In that sublime transaction, as in other miracles,—that the effect might be revealed at once,—the natural time between the cause and the effect was destroyed. What will slowly follow in all men, from the habitual indwelling of God, was brought out for their comfort, before the eyes of the disciples, in a single flash in Christ. The inner life flamed outwards, and glorified, by its outbreaking, the shell which contained it. The 'earthly tabernacle' was dissolved by its heat, and 'the house not made with hands' put on. But to that very condition, up to that very glory of transfigured humanity, every brother and sister of the transfigured Saviour is invited. In them also, in the very humblest of them, a time of transfiguration is drawing on.

Beautiful Soul, whose beauty had come ripening outwards so richly, in this way, through many years, that amid the very shadows of the grave, and when he was standing 'in the vestibule of eternity,' it shone like a light of consolation from heaven :—

'It was this which no one can describe,—it was what the dying man was, that so richly brightened those who, in the darkness of their own sorrow, stood around his bed. . . . The cloud of their grief was irradiated by his sun-like effulgence. . . . For heaven, long since begun in him, was now stealing by imperceptible degrees more and more fully upon him, till heaven just took what it had made all its own. There was so much of heaven begun on earth, that it seemed the most natural of all things that he should pass on to its consummation in its native home. Those who accompanied him, till he gently stepped across the dividing line, felt, in the midst of all their grief, nothing to startle or alarm; and when he went on, they knew the heaven he had gone to, by the heaven he had left behind him.'—*Memoir of the Rev. John Maclaren of Glasgow, by the Rev. Peter Leys of Strathaven*, p. 187.

The spirit of the Saviour is within—'formed within them—the hope of glory.' By daily increase of grace, by daily growth of likeness to the Lord, by daily outbreaking of the light within, by a continual outflow of the formative Holy Spirit,—from the hour of conversion to that of death,—the body will be leavened and new-shaped, and every faculty and feature of its outer life new-formed, until the attributes and character and glory of the transfigured Lord are, in germ at least, impressed upon the entire external personality.

Now this, or the other process has gone on, and is going on, in the depths of all the human life which has been at any hour upon the earth. There has been, and is, in every individual, the destroying force of evil, breaking down what remains of the primal beauty; or the transforming power of the Holy Ghost, building up a new beauty, an image of Christ, amid the very ruins which sin had made. The name written by grace upon the pages of the soul, comes out and displays itself on the pages of the body. The blotting out and the destruction wrought by sin on the inner life, lead to defacement and 'the mark of the beast' without. The actual life we have led, spiritual or unspiritual, writes its exact and perfect story on the outmost surfaces of our being.

IV.

MANIFESTATIONS.

'In that day, a new name, answering to this new condition, shall be put upon us. We have now the name of Christ in the spirit; we are the mystical Christ: then we shall have the name of Christ also in the flesh; we shall be the manifest Christ, shining forth for ever with His glory, and for ever exercising His power, and making His goodness to be known and felt.'—E. IRVING.

WHAT relation death bears to those processes I have been describing, requires no illustration, and hardly any formal statement. It is the termination of possibilities of change, of changes for the better or the worse here. Whether the inner influence has been a debasing or elevating one, at death it ceases. Inward beauty cannot make the body more beautiful; inward defilement cannot make it more impure. 'As the tree falls, so it must lie.' For individuals and generations, and for the whole human race as it descends into the grave, death is the folding up of the great roll of life.

But what, in relation to these changes, is the resurrection from the dead?

IT IS THE JUDICIAL OPENING OF THE BOOK. It is the bringing up into the light again of the buried body. It is more. It is the bringing up to light of the body *changed to its last and abiding form.* 'Thou sowest not that body which shall be, but bare grain.' The dog-spirit sows the dog-body; the swine-spirit the swine-body. The natural man sows the natural body; the Christian sows the sanctified body. Each soul, dead or living, its own body, with all its marks of shame or beauty; of excess or fasting; of hatred or love; of adversity or prosperity; of health or sickness. That is our seed, our sowing in God's acre; and the harvest is the resurrection.

It has been conjectured, as we have already had occasion to state, 'that the change which shall take place in the body, may be itself the appointed means for bringing about a change in the powers and tendencies of the mind.' If this conjecture be—as I think it is—well founded; if this is included in the 'change' to which Paul refers;[1] it would explain, how the frightful revelation which has been made by the bodies of the wicked, and the glorious forms in which the righteous have risen, do not at once, and before everything else, take the attention of that assembled throng. It would explain how 'the books' of memory are appealed to first, and only thereafter, the 'book of life.' The closed doors of the soul are opening, the new senses are putting forth their feelers, the untried functions of the resurrection-mind are hasting into exercise. And by the overpowering influence of the Judge's face (as I have tried to explain in a preceding chapter), all these minds—in their new and completed powers—are thrown back upon themselves, and into the records of their consciousness. But, even without the help which this conjecture supplies, there is explanation enough of the order in which the books are to be opened, in the supreme interest which shall attach to the facts of consciousness, over those which the changed body may

---

[1] 1 Cor. xv. 51, 'And we shall be changed.'

display. Wonderful though the transformation, of which each shall be the subject, and the changes visible in those around, may be, it will be a wonder evoked by an external spectacle. But in that hour, as we may well conceive, the interest shall be withheld from the external, by the more imperious spectacles of the inner life. An interest, nearer and more arresting than even the resurrection body, will be the resurrection, in the memory, of the whole bypast life. All sights, all thoughts, all cares, must give place for the moment to this. One burning interest will throb intensely over the memory-recorded life. One tumultuous agony will press every care aside but one. And then, from within, the terrible or the glad unfolding! Then, on the pictured pages of the memory, the beautiful or the dark reminiscences! Then, the struggle between the evidence and its conclusions; the babbling controversy of the wicked, and the tremulous questionings of the enraptured saints!

The 'books' of memory are opened for this end, that the judged themselves may be satisfied. They repeat into the consciousness of the wicked, the miserable story of their misspent lives; and into the consciousness of the righteous, the sweet experiences of the narrow way. They do most completely lay bare the ground of the condemnation of the wicked. But they are not, and they cannot be, for either class conclusive.

The self-justifying habit of the wicked will lead them to search about for one more refuge of lies; the self-abasing spirit of the righteous will shrink from at once appropriating the full revelation of bliss. The one, accustomed by lies to reply against the claims of their

Maker on the earth, will seek by some new lie to answer the damning evidence of their memories at the judgment-bar; the other, all their lives accustomed to mix trembling with their mirth, without trembling, will not contemplate the dawning glories of their new estate. By both, there will be a turning over of the leaves of memory, a holy and an unholy credulity. Ah, 'Lord! when saw we Thee an hungered, and gave Thee *not* meat?' Ah, 'Lord! when saw we Thee a stranger, and took thee in?' And, from the books within,—from the memories of the judged,—to the book 'written in heaven,' —this 'other book,'—the appeal is made, and the controversy on both sides is closed. The book of life is opened. The evidence, which has been lying before the eye of God and His angels, while the leaves of memory were unfolding, takes now possession of every eye. The lustful discovers himself clothed upon with a body of lust; the avaricious, with a body of avarice; the vain, with a body of vanity; the cruel, with their cruelty; the false, with their falseness; the drunken, with their drunkenness. The inner facts of their consciousness—all that the memory can display—have proclaimed themselves now to the outer eye. He that runneth may read. What was done in the corner, is declared on the housetop. And the eye shrinks and the step falters, and, one by one, out of that shining crowd, each doomed soul is driven by the irresistible pressure of the appalling question,—a question which finds its sting in the black exterior,— 'Friend, how camest *thou* in hither, not having a wedding garment?' And these,—these who are *not* found written in the book of life,—are cast into the lake of fire.

But those who 'fell asleep in Christ' have risen to a higher life. Life has written its new name upon their entire being. The name of the Lamb has expressed itself on their very flesh. The resurrection brings it up to view. 'It was sown in corruption; it is raised in incorruption. It was sown in dishonour; it is raised in glory. It was sown in weakness; it is raised in power. It was sown a natural body; it is raised a spiritual body. For this corruptible must put on incorruption; and this mortal must put on immortality. And when this corruptible shall have put on incorruption, and this mortal shall have put on immortality,' the assembled saints,—in their unity, as the redeemed and risen church; in their distinct personality, as souls which have to answer for themselves, —as they stand in their new adornment before the eye of the Lord, will be the reality and the substance brought out to light, which the symbol of 'the book of life' was intended to portray.

'Come hither, and I will show thee the Bride, the Lamb's wife. And he carried me away in the spirit to a great and high mountain, and showed me that great city, the holy Jerusalem, descending out of heaven from God, having the glory of God. . . . The city had no need of the sun, neither of the moon, to shine in it: for the glory of God did lighten it, and the Lamb is the Light thereof. . . . And the gates of it shall not be shut at all by day: for there shall be no night there. . . . And there shall in no wise enter into it anything that defileth, neither whatsoever worketh abomination, or maketh a lie; but THEY WHO ARE WRITTEN IN THE LAMB'S BOOK OF LIFE.'

V.

THE BIBLE OF THE WORLD TO COME.

'We now see in those around us, that each one has some characteristic feature: in the mind of one we see a deep wisdom; of another, a saintly meekness; of another, an angelic contemplation; of another, a burning charity—each one being a law, a pattern to himself. We see, too, that this characteristic feature is ever coming out into a fuller shape, drawing towards its own perfect idea. So may we believe, that in the kingdom of the resurrection all the gifts of God, all graces of the heart, and all endowments of the sanctified reason, shall then be made perfect; without doubt all that constitutes the mysterious individuality of each several man, all the inscrutable features by which his spiritual being is distinguished, without being opposed to or divided from the spirits of other men, shall be perpetuated hereafter; and then shall all differences be harmonized in the perfection of bliss, as all hues are blended in the unity of light.'
—MANNING.

THERE is yet one more step in this inquiry. May we not enter somewhat into the secret of God's purpose in writing this book of life? Is there not something in the very character of the symbol which we have not touched until we learn this secret?

It is not merely a register of those who have received new names from God. It is not merely an aggregate of names inscribed by life, and inscribed on the entire personality. Those names thus inscribed—expressed in human character, written out in the organs of the body, made manifest by the resurrection, are themselves *thoughts* and *revelations* of the divine mind.

What created thing is not? The under-sea of all existence is the great 'I am.' The trees of the forest draw their life out of God's, and their shapes are expressions of His mind. Of the human framework it is said, in one place,[1] 'that all its members are writ in His book.' They are written there, as the ideas of a poet are written in his poem. And in hill and dale, in cloud and star, we have the evolving stanzas of a mighty poem.

> 'The voice of the Lord is upon the waters,
> The God of glory thundereth. . . .
> The voice of the Lord breaketh the cedars;
> Yea, the Lord breaketh the cedars of Lebanon.'[2]

Yes; and the voice of the Lord causeth the cedar to grow. It is a word, an idea, a thought of His.

Now God puts in His claim to be looked upon as the Author—in the common sense of that word, as well as in a deeper sense—of the life in the regenerate soul, and of the aggregate of all life, in the redeemed and risen Church. 'It is My work,' He says substantially in the Bible; 'the very thought of it is Mine.' It is His, in individual souls; it is His, in the multitude before the throne. And not only the grand result, but every step towards that result—regeneration, sanctification, resurrection, complete redemption. And not the result alone, but the idea, and planning out of the work as well, from its very first beginning. All the growth and realization of spiritual life in individuals, all the outspreading of that life in the Church, all the continuance and progression of

[1] Ps. cxxxix.   [2] Ps. xxix.

it from generation to generation, He claims as His design and handiwork—His only—His from beginning to end.

In connection with this claim of His, what new aspect does 'the book of life' take on for us? What is the object before our minds, when we contemplate the reality which the book symbolizes—the redeemed brought up out of the grave, invested with immortality, and introduced in their new names as citizens of the new Jerusalem?

It is a book written by God—a book filled with His thoughts,—in a most real sense, a *revelation* of God.

And thus at last we are brought, by this as by every other path in the word, to the foot of the cross, and to the blood by which we have been bought. The cross is the grand revealer of the divine heart. But it is not a revelation which began with the Christian era. He who died on the cross was 'the Lamb slain from the foundation of the world.' We must go far back, and far up into the depths of the divine purpose for humanity, to gather the full impression of this fact. Christ's work upon the cross was no expedient to mend a world which had unexpectedly gone wrong. Before the mountains were brought forth, before the earth was formed, Calvary had a place among the purposes of God. Salvation by the blood of the Lamb,—God's wondrous way of peace by grace, and by faith in that blood,—lay defined and clear in the divine plans. Christ crucified was the deep primal thought on which the foundations of the world were laid. Everything arranged itself around this centre. And when human history began, there began beside it, and in the heart of it, a history of the unfolding of this primal thought. Promise followed promise, type was added to type, prophet succeeded prophet, song rose after song, to place a fuller statement of this old thought before the souls of men. The whole history of the Jewish people was a prophet revealing this thought and speaking of Christ,[1] until Christ himself brought, in His sorrow-burdened life and atoning death, the full measure of the truth to light. Do I require here to say, that it is by the truths revealed in this great mystery,—this manifestation of God in the flesh, and this atoning death of the incarnate God,—that the Holy Spirit has been saving souls from the beginning of time? It is because the power of salvation which draws the soul to God, and the formative principle by which Christian character is produced, are equally the truth and life which are in this revelation of the Lamb, that the book is named '*the Lamb's* book of life.' But by this truth and life it is, that souls have been turned to God, and a people realizing and reflecting the divine image gathered out of the world, and built together in Christ.[2] So that, in the retrospect of the history of redemption, to which we may be admitted in eternity,—what we shall see, will be two parallel trails of light. On the one side and from above, we shall see the glorious unfolding, by type and prophecy, of the ancient primal thought—the regenerating and sanctifying truth of

---

[1] Augustine. Confessions. See Note by Dr Pusey. Book iii. cap. 12.—*Lib. Fathers.*

[2] 'Some time ago, a poor Spanish sailor was brought into one of our Liverpool hospitals to die. After he had breathed his last, it was found that over his heart, a rude but indelible representation of Christ on the cross had been made by him, by a process common among seamen. . . . If we could have imprinted *in* our hearts, and in the hearts of all the members of our churches, what that poor

the promised Christ,—dawning and brightening towards the mid-day splendour of the gospel dispensation, revealing, as it advanced into greater fulness, a more perfect image of Him who Himself at length displayed 'the express image' of God, and displayed it 'that He might gather together in one all things in Christ.' And on the other side, we shall see the gathering together of this great unity,—the conversion and building up of the beautiful ones into one temple of beauty, the forming into one combined glory of the individual glories inwrought by grace,—and the growth from generation to generation of a restored humanity, a vast, world-wide, heaven-high image and reproduction of Christ's person and character, redeemed out of every kindred, and people, and tongue, by the blood of the Lamb.

Now, this wondrous unity,—this image of Christ in the combined life of heaven,—is, what Christ Himself is—a revelation of the ways of God, a book disclosing the thoughts of His mind.

We have previously seen, that the 'names' or forms of the redeemed are to be looked upon as ideas and utterances of God. But these individual utterances are not, and cannot be, complete expressions of His mind. Not one soul has gone into His presence, not one soul can ever go, who shall fully body forth the thought incarnate

---

fellow had painfully, and with the needle-point, punctured *over* his, we should soon see success at home and abroad rivalling that of the apostles themselves; for we get to the secret of their wondrous power and pre-eminence when we hear Paul exclaiming, "Alway bearing about in the body the dying of the Lord Jesus, that the life also of Jesus may be made manifest in our body."'—*Rev.* W. M. TAYLOR, M.A., *Bootle. Speech on Missions*, 1865.

in the slain Lamb. One catches and reflects a fragment of it here; one there, another fragment. The attainment of one soul differs from that of another. And the difference consists in this, that the one has what the other wants. What do these wants, these apparent imperfections, in the characters of the godly, point to? They point to this very unity I have been referring to, this one perfection, made up of fragments of perfection. Throughout the Bible, God is presented to us in a waiting attitude. Not only in such expressions as 'He waiteth to be gracious;' but in the impression of that entire portion of our Lord's teaching, which makes mention of an absent Master, whose coming we are to expect. God's people long for their Lord's return. When they see the wickedness in the world, they often ask, 'Why not bring this state of things to a close at once? why delayeth our Lord His coming?' The answer is,—because this work of redeeming mankind is something more than a work of redeeming individual souls. It is a work, which has respect to the combination into one grand unity, of those who shall be redeemed; into one grand book, of all those separate thoughts.

Our fathers loved to think of this unity as a number—the elect number, known to God from the beginning, and which one day would be filled up. The Bible represents it further as a body, a tree, a city, a temple, a new creation, a gathering together into one perfect manhood of all the powers and organs required to body forth a reproduction of himself. The imperfections of which I spoke cease, in the light of this purpose, to be imperfections. They are the separate leaves of the one tree, the separate sentences of the one book of life. What I want, you have; what you want, another has. We are parts of each other; we are to fit in together. Taken together, we are the 'perfect man.' This generation takes an impress of the truth which the last could not receive. That nation attains to a character which no other has reached. The Holy Spirit, applying the truth of the cross, writes, from age to age, syllables and fragments of the divine name on the life of the actual Christendom. Generations, nations, churches, individual souls, each with their special name, their peculiarity, their distinguishing fragment of the divine thought in the word, blend into one at the end. The result of the whole is a full-statured image of our Lord, a complete representation and embodiment, as in a book, of the thoughts in His name. Until the round be completed, until the full height be attained, the Master delayeth His coming. When the last atom shall have gone to its place, His chariot-wheels will revolve.

I seem to myself to be standing now on the inner edges of this mystery. I see facts floating before my mind which were hid from me when I entered. I seem to understand why one generation of God's people is persecuted, and another sent forth to evangelize; why one soul is buried in sorrow, and another lifted into perennial joy. I see life and death, and good and evil, and hope and fear, as the ministers of God, shaping and preparing souls and nations and generations, to take their places in that grand unity, to which the Spirit elsewhere has given the names of the New Creation, and the Perfect Man, but which we have to do with here as 'the book of life.'

And thus we have made entrance into the secret of the divine purpose in this book. The book has a purpose beyond itself. Completed, it will be a new revelation of the divine mind. Its destiny is still further to reveal that mind. It is being filled at this moment with the names of the redeemed,—each name, a thought and utterance of the Divine Author,—that it may take its place in the series of revelations, which God has been bringing forth of himself. What the sentences in the Bible are to its revelation of the Lamb himself, that, the separate realizations of Christian experience and character will be, as thoughts of God, in the Lamb's book of life.

The biographies of men of science have made us acquainted with the pure and high fever of interest, with which the vault of heaven is swept for an expected star. And the humblest of us can enter into their excitement, when the light, which has been hid for millenniums, at last strikes on the mirror of their telescope. Somewhat this may help us to conceive the interest, with which the angels of God,—who have seen coming out upon the bosom of infinity, in stately order, the stars in their courses, and the earth, and man, and higher than all these, the Redeemer of man,—are waiting, even now, in the still expectancy of the upper sanctuary, until the last soul shall be named in the book of life, and the number written 'from the foundation of the world' completed, and humanity's story about God told forth.

And not they alone; other creatures of God as well. God's glorious working shall fill the most distant future, as it has filled the past. New fields for His creative function lie far and near in space. New creations are even now dawning into being. Creations of new worlds may go on for ever. Is it a rash supposal, that—what the shining lights of prophecy, and the cross, and Christ himself, through the Holy Spirit, have been to us,—the embodied array of redeemed humanity, through the same Spirit, may, in some way, be to others? And thus, as *we* have drawn light from revelations of God, in the Old Testament and the New, that we might grow together into one glorified human image of Him, so,—to produce still grander images *in others*,—influences and lights from us may go down the flowing depths of eternity; and 'the book of life,' with its wondrous stories of redeeming love, with its humanly realized thoughts of God, and with its indwelling Christ, be destined to become the Bible of the world to come. 'For God, who is rich in mercy, for His great love wherewith He loved us (even when we were dead in sins), hath quickened us together with Christ, and hath raised us up together, and made us sit in heavenly places in Christ Jesus: That in the ages to come, He might show the exceeding riches of His grace in His kindness toward us though Christ Jesus.' Indeed, for this very end, among others, the Church is gathered into its glorious fellowship: 'That now unto the principalities and powers in heavenly places might be known by the Church the manifold wisdom of God.'[1]

[1] Eph. ii. 4-7, iii. 10. The conclusions are inferential. As the conversion of a single city, or the class represented by that city, in the days of Paul, has been the admiration of the Church ever since, so the conversion of the multitude, which no man can number, may be the wonder of spiritual intelligences throughout the universe for evermore. And as there is such a manifestation of God in this

mystery of redemption, that the instruction derived from it extends beyond the Church on earth, and is shared by the angels in heaven,— angels and intelligences, of orders and worlds different from our own, may continue to find instruction in the study of the thoughts and ways of God, as these shall be displayed in the glorious blood-bought unity represented by the book of life. The following eloquent sentences from Dr Eadie's *Commentary on the Ephesians* exhibit the fact on which the latter inference rests ; but by quoting them I do not presume to suggest, that their author would support the inference :—' The church, which is the scene of these perplexing wonders, teaches the angelic hosts. They have seen much of God's working : many a sun lighted up, and many a world launched into its orbit has delighted them. They have been delighted with the solution of many a problem, and the glorious development of many a mystery. But in the proclamation of the gospel to the Gentiles, with its strange preparations, various agencies, and stupendous effects, involving the origination and extinction of Judaism, the incarnation and atonement, the manger and the cross, the spread of the Greek language, and the triumph of the Roman arms; "these principalities and powers in heavenly places" beheld with rapture other and brighter phases of a wisdom, which had often dazzled them by its brilliant and profuse versatility, and surprised and entranced them by the infinite fulness of the love which prompts it, and of the power which itself directs and controls. The events that have transpired in the Church on earth are the means of augmenting the information of those pure and exalted beings who encircle the throne of God, as may be learned from 1 Tim. iii. 16; 1 Pet. i. 12. The entire drama is at length laid bare before them—

> " Like some bright river, that from fall to fall
> In many a maze descending, bright through all,
> Finds some fair region where, each labyrinth past,
> In one full lake of light it rests at last." '

V.

POSTSCRIPT.

'This body of our Lord hath been carving and working by all the prophets and apostles and ministers, by all the Bezaleels of the world, filled with the Holy Ghost, to this day, limb by limb. . . . When all these shall be brought together, and Christ the Head set upon them, then view them all together, what a sight will it be! Oh, but let me say one thing more. What will it be to be a member of this body, though but the least part of it,—to be one that shall go to make up the fulness of our Lord and Saviour Jesus Christ!'—DR THOMAS GOODWIN.

IT is hardly possible, I suppose, to miss the thought that, on its practical side,—in its present bearing on our life,—'the book of life' is a rich and full symbol of, what we otherwise describe as, *the divine purpose for man in Christ.* To be 'written in heaven,' and to be 'written in the earth,' are the two destinies between which man is placed. He opens his soul to the divine life in the Redeemer, and becomes Christ-like, and linked to all that is fair and holy, and of heaven; or, he shuts out that life, and continues earthly and dead, descending daily to a yet grosser earthliness and state of death, until at length he is an incarnation of the divine wrath.

It is only one of the many shadows of the great mystery of evil, that men are not forward to embrace a life, which carries them nearer to the fulfilment of all the truest and deepest longings of which we are capable. We suffer ourselves to be blinded and misled by the paltry ambitions of Self. The selfish heart will not love a glory, of which God is to be the centre. Its instinct is to dethrone God, and assume His place. To be written in a book, therefore, which draws its inspiration from God, which is filled with His life, and exists to reveal His thoughts, can never be a hope to the unrenewed heart.

The same causes which clog the individual life, retard the progress of the race. The conflict between good and evil lengthens out, because Self and the unrenewed nature dominate in the counsels of social and national life. God is offering us victory, but men will not believe in God. And the Self they confide in, cheats them of their dearest aims, when these seem already in their grasp.

We give swelling names, patched up out of history and prophecy, to the enemy. We call it Papacy, Tyranny, Infidelity, Antichrist. But it is simply Self. This is the soul and essence of all the opposition to good, which is, or ever has been. Antichrist, the Man of Sin, the Wild Beast, which stamps its name on all foreheads that refuse the Lamb's,—it is ever, it is only, Self.

I am describing it, however, from a vantage-ground I cannot occupy in the actual conflict. If Self could be always seen as Self, the danger to the race, or to individuals, would be comparatively small. Its cunning is to enshrine itself behind things venerable and excellent, behind work noble and full of fruit, and fight with other arms than its own. To-day, Ithuriel finds it, as a loathly and venomous thing, at the ear of the human dreamer;

but to-morrow, it is as an angel of God walking by the dreamer's side.

Our plan and dream of life is thus, in many cases, our peril. It has already become our ruin, when the dream is a hope which is without God; a throne on which HE is not to be supreme. The fulfilment of such a dream would be exclusion from the book of life.

And it is an old, old dream, this dream of glorified Self. And it is in every heart, until it is cast out by Christ. And it returns many times to its old haunts, after the Master's 'Come out' has been spoken. It was this very dream, which the Lord saw gleaming in the eyes of the seventy, when they returned to tell Him of their success. 'Lord, even the devils are subject unto us through Thy name.' Unto US! It was a joy to their simple hearts that the devils were subject; but the joy of joys was, that they were subject to *them*.

Not that it is wrong to rejoice in the power and freedom, which the new life brings to us. The wrong thing is to assume to ourselves the glory, which belongs to the giver of this power. A worker stands up to give an account of Christian work. A district has been reclaimed to Christ, or a church has been gathered together, or a long career of teaching has been sustained, or it is an account of revival work, or the report of a missionary society. You can see at once, that the facts are genuine. Great breadths of wickedness have been prevented, or broken up; the domain of righteousness has been extended. But yet you listen with a sickening heart. Every sentence carries you back from the work to the instrument. 'This is *my* nursling!' It was ' speech of *mine*,' or 'plan of *ours*,' which was 'the honoured instrument.' O Lord, how much good we have done! 'The devils are subject unto us.' Listen to the wisdom and foresight of our Lord's reply to the seventy: 'Notwithstanding, in this rejoice not, that the spirits are subject unto you; but rather rejoice because your names are written in heaven.'

It would be only half the truth to say, that there is sin in the ambitions, which report their deeds in this self-glorifying way. But I will say, without danger of exaggeration, that the more of life there is in the heart, the less our reports of work done will terminate on Self. It may be a right thing to aim greatly, to seek to know and do, and be powerful for good. But there is a better thing than even this. It is to be nothing in our own esteem: to be simple recipients of the life which is in Christ; to become thoughts and words of His in the great 'book of life.' This is our true dignity; and until we are able to rejoice in it, and cherish it, we are walking in a vain show, and in the light of the sparks which ourselves have kindled.

Our vocation is to fill the place prepared for us by God. What although the place be humble! If our joy has its root in Christ, and seeks its occasions in His favour, it will seem good to us to occupy even the humblest place. It is the instinct of true life to shrink and give place to the glory of God. 'With twain it covers its face, and with twain it covers its feet.' Meanwhile, we have access into the grace of life, that we may 'rejoice in hope of the glory of God.'

Part Sixth.

MEMORY AND CONSCIENCE.

AN APPENDIX.

' The ancients made Mnemosyne the mother of the Muses, supposing Memory the groundwork and foundation of all skill and learning.'

Abraham Tucker.

' The corruption of our nature has not, directly at least, vitiated our conscience. If it had, our guilt would have been less, and our recovery would have been impossible. For it is through the conscience alone that a fallen, but yet free, intelligence can be reached It is to the conscience that the violated law appeals. It is the conscience that accepts the sentence of condemnation. It is the conscience that pleads guilty of sin as the transgression of the law, and welcomes the assurance of a sufficient expiation.'

Dr Candlish.

I.

THE CONTENTS OF MEMORY.

AUGUSTINE.

'A judgment-book, to fulfil the ends which it has to serve, must contain a full body of evidence, and so arranged as to be easily referred to; a requirement which the memory, and no other faculty of our mind, fulfils.'[1]

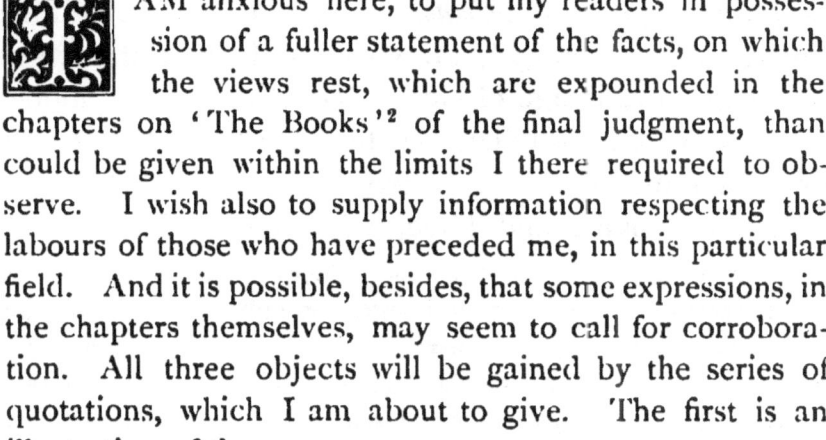AM anxious here, to put my readers in possession of a fuller statement of the facts, on which the views rest, which are expounded in the chapters on 'The Books'[2] of the final judgment, than could be given within the limits I there required to observe. I wish also to supply information respecting the labours of those who have preceded me, in this particular field. And it is possible, besides, that some expressions, in the chapters themselves, may seem to call for corroboration. All three objects will be gained by the series of quotations, which I am about to give. The first is an illustration of the CONTENTS OF MEMORY.

Recent metaphysicians incline to the view which restricts the function of memory to simple *retention*. As I wrote for the general reader, and intended only a popular exposition, I kept, in the chapters referred to above, by

[1] P. 149.   [2] Part Fourth.

the older and larger conception of it, which includes reminiscence, recollection, association of ideas, and trains of thoughts. There is a remarkable passage in the Confessions of Augustine, so illustrative of the mystery of memory, and so little known to common readers, that I give two or three quotations from it here. Much in the same way that Sir William Hamilton represents *Consciousness*, as the deep out of which all mental phenomena arise, Augustine represents *Memory*. It contains for him all knowledge and thought, all virtue and art, and even the knowledge and image of God. To God himself, indeed, he seems to acknowledge, that he must 'pass beyond this power of mine which is called memory; but then,' he adds, 'how shall I find Thee, if I *remember* Thee not?'

'I come to the fields and spacious palaces of my memory, where are the treasures of innumerable images, brought into it from things of all sorts perceived by the senses. There is stored up, whatsoever besides we think, either by enlarging or diminishing, or any other way varying those things which the sense hath come to; and whatever else hath been committed and laid up, which forgetfulness hath not yet swallowed up and buried. When I enter there, I require what I will to be brought forth, and something instantly comes; others must be longer sought after, which are fetched, as it were, out of some inner receptacle; others rush out in troops, and while one thing is desired and required, they start forth, as who should say, "Is it perchance I?" These I drive away with the hand of my heart, from the face of my remembrance, until what I wish for be unveiled, and appear in sight, out of its secret place. Other things come up readily, in unbroken order, as they are called for; those in front making way for the following; and as they make way, they are hidden from sight, ready to come when I will. All which takes place, when I repeat a thing by heart.

'There are all things preserved distinctly and under general heads, each having entered by its own avenue; as light, and all colours and forms of bodies, by the eyes; by the ears, all sorts of sounds; all smells by the avenue of the nostrils; all tastes by the mouth; and by the sensation of the whole body, what is hard or soft, hot or cold, smooth or rugged, heavy or light, either outwardly or inwardly to the body. All these doth that great harbour of the memory receive in her numberless secret and inexpressible windings, to be forthcoming and brought out at need; each entering in by his own gate, and there laid up. Nor yet do the things themselves enter in; only the images of the things perceived, are there in readiness for thought to recall. Which images, how they are formed, who can tell, though it doth plainly appear by which sense each hath been brought in and stored up; for even while I dwell in darkness and silence, in my memory I can produce colours, if I will, and discern betwixt black and white, and what others I will: nor yet do sounds break in and disturb the image drawn in by my eyes, which I am reviewing, though they are also there, lying dormant and laid up, as it were, apart. For these too I call for, and forthwith they appear. And though my tongue be still and my throat mute, so can I sing as much as I will; nor do those images of colours, which notwithstanding be there, intrude themselves and interrupt, when another store is called for, which flowed in by the ears. So the other things piled in and up by the other senses, I recall at my pleasure. Yea, I discern the breath of lilies from violets, though smelling nothing; and I prefer honey to sweet wine, smooth before rugged, at the time neither tasting nor handling, but remembering only.

'These things do I within, in that vast court of my memory. For there are present with me, heaven, earth, sea, and whatever I could think on therein, besides what I have forgotten. There also I meet with myself, and recall myself, and when, where, and what I have done, and under what feelings. There be all which I remember, either on my own experience or others' credit. Out of the same store do I myself with the past continually combine fresh and fresh likenesses of things, which I have experienced, or from what I have experienced have believed; and thence again infer future action, events, and hopes; and all these again I reflect on as present.

'Great is this force of memory, excessive great, O my God; a large and boundless chamber: who ever sounded the bottom thereof?

Yet is this a power of mine, and belongs unto my nature ; nor do I myself comprehend all that I am. . . . Men go abroad to admire the heights of mountains, the mighty billows of the sea, the broad tides of rivers, the compass of the ocean, and the circuits of the stars, and pass themselves by ; nor wonder, that when I spake of all these things, I did not see them with mine eyes, yet could not have spoken of them, unless I then actually saw the mountains, billows, rivers, stars, which I had seen, and that ocean which I believe to be, inwardly in my memory, and that with the same vast spaces between as if I saw them abroad. . . .

'Yet not these alone does the unmeasurable capacity of my memory retain. Here also is all, learnt of the liberal sciences and as yet unforgotten ; removed as it were to some inner place, which is yet no place : nor are they the images thereof, but the things themselves. For what is literature, what the art of disputing, how many kinds of questions there be ? Whatsoever of these I know, in such manner exists in my memory, as that I have not taken in the image, and left out the thing, or that it should have sounded and passed away like a voice fixed on the ear by that impress, whereby it might be recalled, as if it sounded when it no longer sounded. . . . . For those things are not transmitted into the memory, but their images only are, with an admirable swiftness, caught up and stored as it were in wondrous cabinets, and thence wonderfully by the act of remembering, brought forth.

. . . .

. . . 'And how many things of this kind does my memory bear which have been already found out, and, as I said, placed, as it were, at hand, which we are said to have learned and come to know ; which were I for some short space of time to cease to call to mind, they are again so buried, and glide back, as it were, into the deeper recesses, that they must again, as if new, be thought out thence, for other abode they have none. But they must be drawn together again, that they may be known ; that is to say, they must be, as it were, collected together from their dispersion ; whence the word "cogitation" is derived : for *cogo* (collect) and *cogito* (re-collect) have the same relation to each other as *ago* and *agito*, *facio* and *factito*. But the mind hath appropriated to itself this word (cogitation) ; so that, not what is "collected" anyhow, but what is "re-collected," *i.e.* brought together in the mind, is properly said to be cogitated or thought upon. . . .

'Great is the power of memory, a fearful thing, O my God; a deep and boundless manifoldness! And this thing is the mind, and this am I myself. What am I then, O my God? What nature am I? A life various and manifold, and exceedingly immense. Behold in the plains, and caves, and caverns of my memory, innumerable and innumerably full of innumerable kinds of things, either through images, as all bodies; or by actual presence, as the arts; or by certain notions or impressions, as the affections of the mind, which, even when the mind doth not feel, the memory retaineth, while yet whatsoever is in the memory is also in the mind: over all these do I run, I fly; I dive on this side and on that, as far as I can, and there is no end. So great is the force of memory, so great the force of life, even in the mortal life of man. What shall I do then, O thou my true life, my God? I will pass even beyond this power of mine which is called memory; yea, I will pass beyond it, that I may approach unto Thee, O sweet light!'—*Confessions*, Book x.

No one will want any remark on this wonderful passage, or any further illustration of what memory contains; but as I have said, in proof of the fact, that what it contains can be reproduced,—' that the power of association bears the same relation to the contents of memory, which the force of gravitation does to the heavenly bodies,'[1]— I shall adduce in confirmation, the following explanations, by Coleridge, of *the Law of Association*, as set forth by Aristotle:—

'The general law of association, or more accurately, the common condition under which all exciting causes act, and in which they may be generalized according to Aristotle, is this: ideas, by having been together, acquire a power of recalling each other; or, every partial representation awakes the total representation of which it had been

[1] P. 154.

a part. In the practical determination of this common principle to particular recollections, he admits five agents or occasioning causes: 1*st, Connection in time*,—whether simultaneous, preceding, or successive; 2*d, Vicinity*, or connection in space; 3*d, Interdependence*, or necessary connection, as cause and effect; 4*th, Likeness*; 5*th, Contrast*. As an additional solution of the occasional seeming chasms in the continuity of reproduction, he proves that movements or ideas possessing one or the other of these five characters, had passed through the mind as intermediate links, sufficiently clear to recall other parts of the same total impressions with which they had co-existed, though not vivid enough to excite that degree of attention which is requisite for distinct recollection, or, as we may aptly express it, after consciousness. In association, then, consists the whole mechanism of the reproduction of impressions, in the *Aristotelian Psychology*. It is the universal law of the passive fancy and mechanical memory; that which supplies to all other faculties their objects, to all thought the elements of its materials.'—*Biographia Literaria*, vol. i. Part i. chap. vi.

II.

THE IMPERISHABLENESS OF MEMORY.

COLERIDGE AND DE QUINCEY.

'You cannot meet a stranger upon the streets, nor utter a word in your remotest solitude, nor think a thought in your inmost heart, but lo! this Recording Angel has noted it down upon the tablets of your soul for ever.'[1]

FROM the 'contents' of memory I turn to its IMPERISHABLENESS. The illustrations are most interesting, but to me they possess this special charm, that they are, with one or two exceptions, the passages referred to in the preface,—the quotations, by which the esteemed professor commended to his students the view, that memory might be the judgment-book. In the italicised sentence of first quotation the germ of that view will be found:—

'A young woman of four or five and twenty who could neither read nor write was seized with a nervous fever, during which, according to the asseverations of all the priests and monks of the neighbourhood, she became possessed, and, as it appeared, by a very learned devil. She continued incessantly talking Latin, Greek, and Hebrew in very pompous tones, and with most distinct enunciation. . . . The case had attracted the particular attention of a

---

[1] P. 150.

young physician, and by his statement many eminent physiologists and psychologists visited the town and cross-examined the case on the spot. Sheets full of her ravings were taken down from her own mouth, and were found to consist of sentences, coherent and intelligible each for itself, but with little or no connection with each other. Of the Hebrew, a small portion only could be traced to the Bible; the remainder seemed to be in the rabbinical dialect. All trick or conspiracy was out of the question. Not only had the young woman ever been a harmless, simple creature, but she was evidently labouring under a nervous fever. In the town in which she had been resident for many years as a servant in different families, no solution presented itself. The young physician, however, determined to trace her past life step by step; for the patient herself was incapable of returning a rational answer. He at length succeeded in discovering . . . that the patient—an orphan at the time—had been charitably taken by an old Protestant pastor at nine years of age, and had remained with him some years, even till the old man's death. . . . Anxious inquiries were then, of course, made concerning the pastor's habits; and the solution of the phenomenon was soon obtained: for it appeared that it had been the old man's custom for years to walk up and down a passage of his house, into which the kitchen door opened, and to repeat to himself with a loud voice out of his favourite books. . . . He was a very learned man, and a great Hebraist. Among his books (discovered in a niece's possession) were found a collection of rabbinical writings, together with several of the Greek and Latin fathers; and the physician succeeded in identifying so many passages with those taken down at the young woman's bedside, that no doubt could remain in any rational mind concerning the true origin of the impression made on her nervous system.

'This authenticated case furnishes both proof and instance, that reliques of sensation may exist for an indefinite time in a latent state, in the very same order in which they were originally impressed; and as we cannot rationally suppose the feverish state of the brain to act in any other way than as a *stimulus*, this fact (and it would not be difficult to adduce several of the same kind) contributes to make it even probable, that all thoughts are in themselves imperishable;

and that, if the intelligent faculty should be rendered more comprehensive, *it would require only a different and apportioned organization—the body celestial instead of the body terrestrial—to bring before every human soul the collective experience of its whole past existence. And this—this—perchance is the dread book of judgment, in the mysterious hieroglyphics of which every idle word is recorded.* Yea, in the very nature of a living spirit, it may be more possible that heaven and earth should pass away, than that a single act, a single thought, should be loosened or lost from that living chain of causes, with all the links of which, conscious or unconscious, the free will, our only absolute self, is co-extensive and co-present.'— COLERIDGE: *Biographia Literaria*, vol. i., First Part, chap. vi.

After the death of Professor John Wilson, Mr Warren published an account of an interview he once had with the Professor, when Mr De Quincey was present, and the conversation happened to turn on 'forgetting.'

'"Is such a thing as *forgetting* possible to the human mind?" asked Mr De Quincey. "Does the mind ever actually lose anything for ever? Is not every impression it has once received reproducible? How often a thing is suddenly recollected that had happened many, many years before, but never been thought of since till that moment! Possibly a suddenly developed power of recollecting every act of a man's life, may constitute the great book to be opened before Him on the judgment-day." I ventured to say, that I knew an instance of a gentleman who, in hastily jumping on board the "Excellent," ... missed it, and fell into the water of Portsmouth harbour, sinking to a great depth. For a while he was supposed drowned. He afterwards said, that all he remembered after plunging into the water, was a sense of freedom from pain, and a sudden recollection of all his past life, especially of guilty actions that he had long forgotten. Professor Wilson said, that if this were so, it was indeed very startling; and I think Mr De Quincey said, that he also had heard of one, if not of two or three, such cases.'—'Personal Recollections of Christopher North,' *Blackwood's Magazine*, Dec. 1851.

This extract from *Blackwood's Magazine* may serve as an appropriate introduction to a passage from Mr De Quincey's own writings,—a passage which cannot fail to suggest, what the subject, which those quotations are intended to illustrate, might have become in the hands of a master. It is from his well-known description of the *Palimpsest of the Brain* :—

'The fleeting accidents of man's life, and its external shows, may indeed be irrelate and incongruous; but the organizing principles which fuse into harmony, and gather about fixed predetermined centres, whatever heterogeneous elements life may have accumulated from without, will not permit the grandeur of human unity greatly to be violated, or its ultimate repose to be troubled in the retrospect from dying moments, or from other great convulsions. Such a convulsion is the struggle of gradual suffocation, as in drowning; and in the original Opium Confessions, I mentioned a case of that nature communicated to me by a lady from her own childish experience. The lady is still living; and at the time of relating this incident, when already very old, she had become religious to scepticism. According to my present belief, she had completed her ninth year, when, playing by the side of a solitary brook, she fell into one of its deepest pools. Eventually, but after what lapse of time nobody ever knew, she was saved from death by a farmer, who, riding in some distant lane, had seen her rise to the surface; but not until she had descended within the abyss of death, and looked into its secrets, as far, perhaps, as ever human eye *can* have looked that had permission to return. At a certain stage of this descent, a blow seemed to strike her—phosphoric radiance sprang forth from her eyeballs; and immediately a mighty theatre expanded within her brain. In a moment, in the twinkling of an eye, every act, every design of her past life, lived again—arraying themselves, not as a succession, but as parts of a co-existence. Such a light fell upon the whole path of her life backwards into the shades of infancy, as the light, perhaps, which wrapt the destined apostle on his road to Damascus. Yet that light blinded for a season; but hers poured celestial vision upon the brain, so that her consciousness became omnipresent at one moment to every feature in the infinite review. This anecdote was treated sceptically at the time by some critics. But, besides that it has since been confirmed by other experiences essentially the same, reported by other parties in the same circumstances who had never heard of each other, the true point for astonishment is not the *simultaneity* of arrangement under which the past events of life—though in fact successive—had formed their dread line of revelation. This was but a secondary phenomenon; the deeper lay in the resurrection itself, and the possibility of resurrection for what had so long slept in the dust. A pall, deep as oblivion, had been thrown by life over every trace of these experiences; and yet suddenly, at a silent command, at the signal of a blazing rocket sent up from the brain, the pall draws up, and the whole depths of the theatre are exposed. Here was the greater mystery. Now this mystery is liable to no doubt; for it is repeated, and ten thousand times repeated, by opium, for those who are its martyrs. Yes, reader, countless are the mysterious handwritings of grief or joy which have inscribed themselves successively upon the palimpsest of your brain; and like the annual leaves of aboriginal forests, or the undissolving snows on the Himalaya, or light falling upon light, the endless strata have covered up each other in forgetfulness. But by the hour of death, but by fever, but by the scorchings of opium, all these can revive in strength. They are not dead, but sleeping.'

The case of drowning in Portsmouth harbour, referred to in the conversation at Professor Wilson's, is familiar enough to students of mental philosophy, but I give it here for the sake of the general reader. Apart from its value as an illustration of the imperishableness of thought, it is intrinsically worth repeating. The writer was Admiral Beaufort, and the narrative was drawn up (in 1825) at the request of Dr Wollaston, to whom the substance of it had been communicated orally some time before.

After giving the details of the falling into the water, and the preparations for rescuing him, the narrator states:—

'With the violent but vain attempts to make myself heard, I had swallowed much water; I was soon exhausted by my struggles, and before any relief reached me I had sunk below the surface: all hope had fled—all exertion ceased—and I *felt* I was drowning. So far, these facts were either partially remembered after my recovery, or supplied by those who had latterly witnessed the scene; for during an interval of such agitation a drowning person is too much occupied in catching at every passing straw, or too much absorbed by alternate hope and despair, to mark the succession of events very accurately.

'Not so, however, with the facts which immediately ensued: my mind had then undergone the sudden revolution which appeared to you so remarkable, and all the circumstances of which are now as vividly fresh in my memory as if they had occurred but yesterday. From the moment that all exertion had ceased, which I imagine was the immediate consequence of complete suffocation, a calm feeling of the most perfect tranquillity superseded the previous tumultuous sensations; it might be called apathy, certainly not resignation, for drowning no longer appeared to be an evil. I no longer thought of being rescued, nor was I in any bodily pain. On the contrary, my sensations were now of rather a pleasurable cast, partaking of that dull but contented sort of feeling which precedes the sleep produced by fatigue. Though the senses were thus deadened, not so the mind: its activity seemed to be invigorated, in a ratio which defies all description; for thought rose after thought with a rapidity of succession that is not only indescribable, but probably inconceivable by any one who has not himself been in a similar situation. The course of those thoughts I can even now in a great measure retrace: the event which had just taken place—the awkwardness that had produced it —the bustle it must have occasioned (for I had observed two persons jump from the chains)—the effect it would have on a most affectionate father—the manner in which he would disclose it to the rest of the family—and a thousand other circumstances minutely associated with home, were the first series of reflections that occurred. They then took a wider range: our last cruise—a former voyage and shipwreck—my school, the progress I had made there, and the time I had misspent—and even all my boyish pursuits and adventures.

'Thus travelling backwards, every past incident of my life seemed to glance across my recollection in retrograde succession ; not, however, in mere outline, as here stated, but the picture filled up with every minute and collateral feature : in short, the whole period of my existence seemed to be placed before me in a kind of panoramic review, and each act of it seemed to be accompanied by a consciousness of right or wrong, or by some reflection on its cause or its consequences ; indeed, many trifling events which had been long forgotten then crowded into my imagination, and with the character of recent familiarity.

'May not all this be some indication of the almost infinite power of memory with which we may awaken in another world, and thus be compelled to contemplate our past lives ? Or might it not in some degree warrant the inference that death is only a change or modification of our existence, in which there is no real pause or interruption ? But however that may be, one circumstance was highly remarkable : that the innumerable ideas which flashed into my mind were all retrospective. Yet I had been religiously brought up: my hopes and fears of the next world had lost nothing of their early strength, and at any other period intense interest and awful anxiety would have been excited by the mere probability that I was floating on the threshold of eternity ; yet at that inexplicable moment, when I had a full conviction that I had already crossed that threshold, not a single thought wandered into the future: I was wrapt entirely in the past.

'The length of time that was occupied by this deluge of ideas, or rather the shortness of time into which they were condensed, I cannot now state with precision ; yet certainly two minutes could not have elapsed from the moment of suffocation to that of my being hauled up.'—*Letter from Admiral Beaufort to Dr Wollaston, in Sir J. Barrow's Autobiography*, pp. 398–401.

One instance more. When the 'Central America' was wrecked in 1857, those who were ultimately saved floated about for hours, clinging to planks and life-preservers, and seem to have experienced even more than the horrors of death. It was night, and the fear of sharks took possession of them. In these circumstances, a little shred of past life and early guilt—forgotten—unthought of for twenty years—forced itself upon the mind of one of the survivors. The homely style of the narrative deducts nothing from the illustrative worth of what he tells:—

'I guess I had been about four hours in the water, and had floated away from the rest, when the waves ceased to make any noise, and I heard my mother say, "Johnny, did you eat sister's grapes?" I hadn't thought of it for twenty years at least. It had gone clean out of my mind. I had a sister that died of consumption, more than thirty years ago; and when she was sick—I was a boy of eleven or so—a neighbour had sent her some early hothouse grapes. Well, those grapes were left in a room where I was, and—I ought to have been skinned alive for it, little rascal that I was—I devoured them all. Mother came to me after I had gone to bed, when she couldn't find the fruit for sister to moisten her mouth with in the night, and said, "Johnny, did you eat sister's grapes?" I did not add to the meanness of my conduct by telling a lie. I owned up, and my mother went away in tears, but without flogging me. It occasioned me a qualm of conscience for many a year after; but, as I said, for twenty years at least I had not thought of it, till when I was floating about benumbed with cold I heard it as plain as ever I heard her voice in my life: I heard mother say, "Johnny, did you eat sister's grapes?" I don't know how to account for it. Although it did not scare me, I thought it was a presage of my death.'—*Newspaper of the time.*

The readers of Locke will recall the well-known passage where the opposite phenomenon of decay of memory is given in language as beautiful as it is clear:—

'The ideas, as well as children, of our youth, often die before us; and our minds represent to us those tombs to which we are approaching, where, though the brass and marble remain, yet the inscriptions are effaced by time, and the imagery moulders away. The pictures drawn in our minds are laid in fading colours, and if not sometimes refreshed, vanish and disappear. How much the constitution of our bodies, and the make of our animal spirits, are concerned in this, and whether the temper of the brain makes this difference, that in some it retains the characters drawn on it like marble, in others like freestone, and in others little better than sand, I shall not here inquire; though it may seem probable that the constitution of the body does sometimes influence the memory, since we oftentimes find a disease quite strip the mind of all its ideas, and the flames of a fever in a few days calcine all those to dust and confusion which seemed to be as lasting as if engraved in marble.'

But no one more readily than Locke himself would explain that this history of decay did not extend beyond the grave. To him the resurrection-life was a blessed hope. And apart from this, as I well remember my old professor saying, when quoting this passage, 'What rises again is not the material body or brain which influences the memory here, but the spiritual body with all its inalienable facts of acquirement and character.' The resurrection is the reproduction not only of the life and personality of earth, but of all the inscriptions engraved on their surface—indelible thenceforth for ever.

III.

REMEMBERING IN THE FUTURE.

JEREMY AND ISAAC TAYLOR.

'Up from her profoundest depths will arise the long-forgotten and unconfessed iniquities.'[1]

WHATEVER of worth there may be, in viewing the judicial instruments of the present and the future in their organic unity; or in suggesting a method by which, through the operation of existing laws, the secrets of memory may be disclosed on the day of judgment, there is neither merit nor novelty in reproducing the fact, that the remembrances of the judged will play an important part among the processes and events of that day. The subject has always been a favourite one with preachers, and, among others, has received large and rich illustration from the English divines of the seventeenth century, and their American and Scotch successors of the eighteenth. The usual purpose of their illustrations, however, is to exhibit the nature of the future woe. The 'remembering' they dwell upon and unfold, is the remembering of the doomed in hell. Jeremy Taylor is an exception. In his three great sermons on 'Christ's Advent to Judgment,' he has not failed to notice and mark out the part, which memory has

[1] P. 168.

to play, while the wicked are still before the throne. My immediate object is to quote the particular paragraph of the sermon in which this is done; but as the sweep of that and its companion discourses covers a large portion of the field I have been traversing, I shall enrich these pages with two additional paragraphs,—the one illustrative of the prelusive character of the judgments of Providence, the other of the appearance of the Judge :—

'We may guess at the severity of the Judge by the lesser strokes of that judgment which He is pleased to send upon sinners in this world, to make them afraid of the horrible pains of doom's-day : I mean the torments of an unquiet conscience, the amazement and confusions of some sins and some persons. For I have sometimes seen persons surprised in a base action, and taken in the circumstances of crafty theft and secret injustices, before their excuse was ready. They have changed their colour, their speech hath faltered, their tongue stammered, their eyes did wander and fix nowhere, till shame made them sink into their hollow eye-pits to retreat from the images and circumstances of discovery; their wits are lost, their reason useless : the whole order of the soul is discomposed, and they neither see, nor feel, nor think as they use to do; but they are broken into disorder by a stroke of damnation and a lesser stripe of hell.'

Touching the appearing of the Lord, he has many things to say; but this, bearing on the *effect* of His appearing on the wicked, is the most pertinent to my purpose here :—

'How shalt thou look upon Him that fainted and died for love of thee, and thou didst scorn His miraculous mercies ? How shall we dare to behold that holy face that brought salvation to us, and we turned away and fell in love with death, and kissed deformity and sins ! And yet in the beholding of that face consists much of the glories of eternity ! All the pains and passions, the sorrows and the groans, the humility and poverty, the labours and the watchings, the prayers and the sermons, the miracles and the prophecies, the whip and the nails, the death and the burial, the shame and the smart, the cross and the grave of Jesus, shall be laid upon thy score, if thou hast refused the mercies and design of all their holy ends and purposes.'

Coming to the working of memory and conscience in the day of judgment, he says :—

'As our conscience will represent all our sins to us, so the Judge will represent all His Father's kindnesses, as Nathan did to David when he was to make the justice of the divine sentence appear against him. Then it shall be remembered that the joys of every day's piety would have been a greater pleasure every night, than the remembrance of every night's sin could have been in the morning. . . . The offering ourselves to God every morning, and the thanksgiving to God every night, hope and fear, shame and desire, the honour of leaving a fair name behind us, and the shame of dying as a fool,—everything, indeed, in the world is made to be an argument and inducement to us to invite us to come to God and be saved ; and, therefore, when this and infinitely more shall by the Judge be exhibited in sad remembrances, there needs no other sentence : we shall condemn ourselves with a hasty shame and a fearful confusion, to see how good God hath been to us, and how base we have been to ourselves. . . . .

'*Our conscience shall be our accuser.* But this signifies but these two things : *first*, that we shall be condemned for the evils that we have done, and shall then remember,—God by His power wiping away the dust from the tables of our memory, and taking off the consideration and the voluntary neglect, and rude shuffling of our cases of conscience; for then we shall see things as they are, the evil circumstances and the crooked intentions, the adherent unhandsomeness and the direct crimes : for all things are laid up safely ; and though we draw a curtain of a cobweb over them, and sew figleaves before our shame, yet God shall draw away the curtain, and forgetfulness shall be no more, because, with a taper in the hand of God, all the corners of our nastiness shall be discovered. And, *second*, it signifies this also, that not only the justice of God shall be confessed by us in our own shame and condemnation; but the evil of the sentence shall be received into us to melt our bowels, and to break our hearts in pieces within us, because we are the authors of our own death, and our own inhuman hands have torn our souls in pieces.'

When these words were written, it was still usual to look upon the body as a clog upon the mind, a sort of prison-house from which death would set us free. The great truth that the body is the instrument of the mind, and that death and resurrection are the passing upward into the possession of a more perfect instrument—the *body celestial*, instead of the *body terrestrial*—had to wait another century and a half, before it could be received into the Christian psychology of England. But it may serve to mark at once the advancement towards more exact views on this subject, which Christian philosophy has attained, since the days of the great Royalist preacher; and the nearness to the full truth, which (without this exactitude) Taylor reached, if, before quoting the passage I am about to extract from *The Physical Theory of Another Life* of his illustrious namesake, I give one other paragraph from the sermon which has supplied the preceding quotations :—

'The evils of this world are material and bodily: the pressing of a shoulder, or the straining of a joint; the dislocation of a bone, or the extending of an artery; a bruise in the flesh, or the pinching of the skin; a hot liver, or a sickly stomach; and then the mind is troubled because its instrument is ill at ease. But all the proper troubles of this life are nothing but the effects of an uneasy body, or an abused fancy, and therefore can be no bigger than a blow or a cosenage, than a wound or a dream; only the trouble increases as the soul works it; and if it makes reflex acts, and begins the evil upon its own account, then it multiplies and doubles, because the proper scene of grief is opened, and sorrow peeps through the corners of the soul. But in those regions and days of sorrow, when the soul shall be no more depending upon the body, but the perfect principle of all its actions, the actions are quick and the perceptions brisk; the passions are extreme, and the motions are spiritual; the pains are like the horrors of a devil, and the groans of an evil spirit; not slow like the motions of a heavy foot, or a loaden arm; but quick as an angel's wing, active as lightning; and a grief *then* is nothing like a grief *now;* and the words of a man's tongue which are fitted to the uses of this world, are as unfit to signify the evils of the next, as *person*, and *nature*, and *hand*, and *motion*, and *passion* are to represent the effects of the divine attributes, actions, and subsistence.'

In the course of the great work I have already named —*The Physical Theory of Another Life*—Isaac Taylor comes upon this very theme. But he handles it in illustration of the new experiences of a soul clothed with the resurrection body. Substantially, the conclusions are the same. But where, in the earlier writer, the conclusion is reached through the conviction, that *then* 'the soul shall be no more depending on the body;' in the later, it is reached through the fact, that the soul will have a fuller and more exquisite instrument in the resurrection body than it has at present. Among the changes which may be supposed to be effected on the powers of the mind, by the new corporeal structure, the changes on memory are noted as pre-eminent. The chapter in which these changes are described, has so direct a bearing on the discussions in that part of my volume to which these pages are meant as an appendix, that I make no apology for quoting the greater portion of it here.

'The memory is, in a peculiar sense, a function of the brain; and as, in the admission of images of the external world, everything depends upon the sensorium, so likewise in the retention and the reproduction of these ideas, the physical structure and the actual condition or healthy action of the cerebral organ determine its power and its activity. The memory grows with the growth of the body, strengthens with adolescence, is the contemporary of animal energy; and is the first of the mental powers to betray the incipient decay of the vital force: the grey head, the impaired sight, the trembling limb, and the faithless memory, tell of the advance of years, even while reason, and perhaps imagination, scarcely seem to decline. Again, it is the memory that is the most directly affected by external injuries of the head, or by those diseases that spend their violence upon the brain. It is the memory, moreover, that asks for, and admits, those artificial aids which bespeak its intimate alliance with corporeal impressions. Thus it is that any very peculiar physical sensation, recurring after a long interval, brings to our recollection the incidental circumstances and the mental state at the time of its first occurrence. . . .

'It is therefore obvious that this organic mental faculty, as at present possessed even by the most highly favoured individuals, is susceptible of much enhancement and extension, merely by an improvement of the corporeal constitution. . . .

'As sensation is a limited consciousness of the external world, so is memory a limited and incidental recollection of our past states of feeling: it is a partial exercise of a larger power, which, in adapting itself to the occasions of active life, forfeits or holds in abeyance its plenary prerogatives. Considered as a function of the brain, the memory retains what it retains, and reproduces what it reproduces, according to the law of an arbitrary, and often accidental, connection of ideas. The power which, in its original capacity, might have filled a broad field, does in fact only beat a narrow path, and gropes its way backward over the ground it has traversed, in search of what it has dropped. Or, to change our comparison, the memory is a book, the blank leaves of which are constantly filling, but of which the written portion never lies outspread before us; and, moreover, the paper being of frail texture, and the ink evanescent, and the entries often made in haste, or carelessly, they soon become totally illegible. . . .

'Perhaps, if our impressions of the past were not in some such manner liable to be abated and borne down, or obscured and obliterated, there would, in most minds, be certain vivid recollections which would continue to usurp the entire consciousness, and so exclude the present, with its fainter sensations, its interests and its duties; and we might thus be liable to long seasons of abstraction, during which we should stand like statues amid the urgent affairs of the passing moment. Such, in fact, is the misfortune of a class of morbid minds. But this necessity for abating the vividness of the memory is temporary only; and it is easy to imagine such an enhancement of the active force of the mind, in relation to the passing moment, as should fully counterpoise the influence of even the most distinct and vivid recollection of scenes gone by. Let but the voluntary principle be proportionately invigorated, and then the mind might enjoy a permanent and bright consciousness of all that it has ever known, felt, and performed :—it might thus repossess itself of its entire past existence, and might continue to enjoy (or to endure) an ever-growing and entire recollection of its various successive states: it might every moment live its whole life over simultaneously, and with infallible accuracy might be conscious of all the circumstances and shades of every portion of its being. However much such a full consciousness of the past might seem to exceed, in kind as well as in amount, our present partial and fallacious recollections, it would nevertheless be only the same power of the mind, set free from physical obstructions and infirmities. . . .

'The spiritual body, in itself indestructible and exempt from the liability to animal decay, may allow the mental faculty to spread itself out to the full; as if an inscription, which heretofore had been committed to a leaf, or papyrian scroll, was now transferred to a fair and ample surface of Parian marble. . . .

'The moral life is, in a peculiar sense—A HISTORY: it is a process, involving successive stages, through the course of which the unalterable laws of the spiritual economy are in turn brought to bear upon the dispositions and conduct of those who are subject thereto. Take away memory, and we go near to annul government and to destroy accountability.

'Now it is as *embodied*, and as thereby conversant with material objects, that the mind learns to arrange its consciousness in a series, or in other words, exercises memory. For this faculty, although not exclusively conversant with material objects, yet rarely, if ever, entertains any notions, as constituting part of our past history, unless connected with things seen, heard, and felt. Pure abstract conceptions may indeed keep their place in the mind; but whenever the having entertained such conceptions is *remembered*, it is only as they may have been accidentally conjoined with circumstances of place or company, or with physical sensations. The memory leans upon the material world.

'On both these accounts then,—that is to say, first, because it is peculiarly dependent upon the bodily organization; and secondly, because it is mainly conversant with images of the external world,—the faculty of memory is one which, with the highest probability, we may expect to be greatly extended and improved in a new and a more refined corporeal structure. . . .

'A little steady reflection will open to any one who pursues the idea, many momentous consequences involved in the supposition of an entire continuous recollection of our past existence, or of what might be termed a PLENARY MEMORY. In relation to the maturing of the moral life, it is this vivid consciousness of the whole series of our actions and emotions, that is needed for penetrating the mind with a sense of its own condition, and for rendering it its own equitable censor. It is manifest that those egregiously false estimates, which we so often entertain of our own merits, gain entrance by favour of an oblivion of the most considerable and characteristic portions of our moral life. It is from a full and incessant recollection of the past, that are to arise, if at all, and in a due and necessary intensity, those strivings of the spirit with itself, and those compunctious agonies of the heart, whence improvement may result. The trite motto on a sun-dial, *Non sine lumine*, might aptly be transferred to the human conscience in relation to memory; and we may believe that when its full light, unabated and perpetual, shall be brought to bear upon the soul's sense of good and evil, then shall be developed, in its dread power, the force of the moral principle as implanted by God in our bosoms.

'The abstract possibility of an entire restoration of memory, or of the recovery of the whole that it has ever contained, need not be questioned; or if it were, an appeal might be made to every one's personal experience: for we suppose there are none to whom it has not happened to have a sudden recollection—a flashing of some minute and unimportant incident of early life or childhood; and perhaps after an interval of forty or sixty years. With some persons, these unconnected and uncalled for reminiscences are frequent, and very vivid; and they seem to imply that, although the mind may have lost its command over the stores of memory, and may no longer be able to recall at will the remote passages of its history, yet that the memory itself has not really parted with any of its deposits, but holds them faithfully (if not obediently) in reserve, against a season when the whole will be demanded of it. Might not the human memory be compared to a field of sepulture, thickly stocked with the remains of many generations; but of all these thousands whose dust heaves the surface, a few only are saved from immediate oblivion upon tablets and urns; while the many are, at present, utterly lost to knowledge. Nevertheless each of the dead has left in that soil an imperishable germ; and all, without distinction, shall another day start up, and claim their dues.'

IV.

CONSCIENCE.

DR WHEWELL.

'Be that knowledge great or small, it is, to the extent of it, our law of God; and this law our conscience has in charge.'[1]

FOR the reason referred to already, because the chapter in which these words occur, originally formed part of a lecture prepared for a general audience, my description of conscience, and the relation it bears to memory, did not and could not aim at much precision. Partly to supply a better description, partly to corroborate the views I have advanced regarding the connection between the Word in the keeping of conscience and the face of the Judge, I quote here some passages from the writings of one of the most illustrious living expositors of moral science in England :—

'We approve or disapprove of what we have done or tried to do. We consider our acts, external and internal, with reference to a moral standard of right and wrong. We recognise them as virtuous or vicious. The faculty or habit of doing this is conscience.

'As *science* means *knowledge*, *conscience* etymologically means *self-knowledge;* and such is the meaning of the word in Latin and French, and of the corresponding word in Greek (*conscientia*, conscience, συνιδησις). But the English word implies a moral standard of action in the mind, as well as a consciousness of our own actions. It may be convenient to us to mark this distinction of an internal

[1] P. 160.

moral standard as one part of conscience; and self-knowledge, or consciousness, as another part. The one is the internal law, the other the internal accuser, witness, and judge. This distinction was noted by early Christian moralists. They termed the former part of conscience *synteresis*, the internal repository; the latter *syneidesis*, the internal knowledge. We may term the former conscience as law, the latter conscience as witness. . . . The offices of conscience as witness, accuser, and judge, cannot easily be separated; for to be conscious of having done an act, to question its character, and to know that it is wrong, are steps which usually follow close upon each other. Yet these steps may often be distinct. It may require some consideration, and some careful exercise of the intellect, to discern the important features of an act, and to apply to it the appropriate rules of duty. The moralists who distinguish the *synteresis* from the *syneidesis*, represent the acts of conscience as expressed by the three members of a syllogism, of which the first contains the *law;* the second, the *witness;* the third, the *judgment.* As an example, we may take this syllogism: He who dissembles, transgresses the duty of truth; I have dissembled; therefore I have transgressed the duty of truth. We may also note a further office which is ascribed to conscience. She inflicts *punishment* for the offences thus condemned; for the self-accusation and self-condemnation, of which we have spoken, bring with them their especial pains. Repentance is sorrow; remorse is a pang, a torment; transgression lies like a weight on the conscience, and makes it feel burthened and oppressed. Again, the conscience is spoken of as the record of offences committed; and as stained, polluted, blackened by our transgressions.

'Conscience, the judge, must pronounce its decision according to conscience, the law. If we have not transgressed the law of conscience, conscience acquits us. If we have violated the law of conscience, conscience condemns us.

'He who is condemned by his own conscience is guilty. He has really done wrong. He has really offended against the supreme rule. His actions are inconsistent with the stage at which he has arrived in his moral progress. They are therefore inconsistent with morality. He who acts *against his conscience* is always wrong.

'The question naturally occurs, whether, on the other hand, he who acts *according to his conscience* is always right; whether he who is acquitted by his conscience is free from blame. Is it enough for the demands of morality, if each person compares his actions to the standard of right and wrong which he has in his mind? Is this a complete justification?

'It is evident, that to answer these questions in the affirmative would lead to great inconsistencies in our morality; for, under the influence of education, laws, prejudices, and passions, the standard of right and wrong, which exists in men's minds for the time, is often very different from that which the moralist can assent to. Men have often committed thefts, frauds, impositions, homicides, thinking their actions right, though they were such as all moralists would condemn as wrong. Such men acted according to their consciences. Were they thereby justified?

'What has already been said, may suggest a reply to such questions. It is the duty of man constantly to prosecute his moral and intellectual culture. This requires not only that we should conform our actions to the standard which we have in our minds for the time; but that also we are to make this standard truly moral. Whatever subordinate law we have in our minds, is to be looked upon only as a step to the supreme law—the law of complete benevolence, justice, truth, purity, and order. Conscience, the law, must be constantly directed with the purpose of making it conform to this supreme law. We must seek for such light, such knowledge, as may enable us constantly to promote this conformity. We must labour to *enlighten* and *instruct* our conscience. This task can never be ended. So long as life and powers of thought remain to us, we may always be able to acquire a still clearer and higher view than we yet possess of the supreme law of our being. We never can have done all that is in our power in this respect. It never can be consistent with our duty to despair of enlightening and instructing our conscience beyond what we have yet done. Our standard of virtue is not high enough, if we think it need be made no higher. Virtue has never so completely taken possession of man's being, but that she may possess it still more completely; and, therefore, any conception of virtue which we look upon as perfect, must on that very account be imperfect.

Conscience is never fully formed, but always in the course of formation. We may add, that in attempting to enlighten and instruct our conscience, and to carry on our moral progress, we are led to feel the want of some light and some power in addition to the light of mere reason, and the ordinary powers which we possess over our own minds; and that religion offers to us the hope of such a power, which will, if duly sought, be exercised upon us.'—*Dr Whewell's Elements of Morality*, vol. i. chap. xiv.

V.

EXTERNAL TESTIMONY.

BABBAGE.

'No separate or outward Book needs to be produced.'[1]

THERE have been many ingenious speculations on the *External proofs* of sin which may be adduced on the judgment-day. Mr Babbage, in his *Ninth Bridgewater Treatise*,—giving a moral application to a mechanical principle,—maintains, that the very air which surrounds us, the water on which we sail, the earth we tread, will preserve memorials of guilty deeds. Not a sound which passes from human lips but leaves its impression on the air; not a pebble thrown into a lake, but produces a result which goes on for ever:—

'The air itself is one vast library, on whose pages are for ever written all that man has ever said, or even whispered. There, in their mutable but unerring characters, mixed with the earliest as well as the latest sighs of mortality, stand for ever recorded vows unredeemed, promises unfulfilled, perpetuating in the united movements of each particle the testimony of man's changeful will.'

As in air, so in water:—

'No motion, impressed by natural causes or by human agency, is ever obliterated. . . . The track of every canoe, of every vessel

[1] P. 172.

which has yet disturbed the surface of the ocean, whether impelled by manual force or elemental power, remains for ever registered in the future movement of all succeeding particles which may occupy its place. The furrow which it left is indeed instantly filled up by the closing waters; but they draw after them other and larger portions of the surrounding element, and these again once moved, communicate motion to others in endless succession. . . .

'If the Almighty stamped on the brow of the earliest murderer the indelible and visible mark of his guilt, He has also established laws by which every succeeding criminal is not less irrevocably chained to the testimony of his crime; for every atom of his mortal frame, through whatever changes its severed particles may migrate, will still retain, adhering to it through every combination, some movement derived from the muscular effort by which the crime itself was perpetrated.'

We cannot see those hidden and silent records, but the Omniscient can. And, as Mr Babbage, with great eloquence, goes on to say, in a higher sphere there may be inlets of perception even to ourselves,—

'Acute enough to trace the impression through all its bearings, and thus render every atom of the globe a living witness to the actions of every living being. And thus it may happen, to take a single illustration, that the soul of the negro, whose fettered body, surviving the living charnel-house of his infected prison, was thrown into the sea to lighten the ship (that his master might escape the limited justice assigned by society to crimes here), will need, at the last great day of human accounts, no living witness of his earthly agony. When man and all his race shall have disappeared from the face of our planet, ask every particle of air still floating over the unpeopled earth, and it will record the cruel mandate of the tyrant. Interrogate every wave which breaks unimpeded on ten thousand desolate shores, and it will give evidence of the last gurgle of the waters which closed over the head of his dying victim. Confront the murderer with every corporeal atom of his immolated slave, and in its still quivering movements he will read the prophet's denunciation of the Hebrew king.'—BABBAGE: *Ninth Bridgewater Treatise*, pp. 114, 117.

Dr Hitchcock, in his '*Religion and Geology*,' refers to other writers who have amplified this speculation, and carried it along the new lines, which have been opened up to us by the recent discoveries in optics, electricity, and photography. As Mr Babbage fancied the universe a sounding gallery, those others have supposed, that it is also a vast picture gallery, where the sun is every moment photographing the actions of men, and the sunlight conveying those photographs to the walls of some future dwelling-place of the human race :—

'Thus,' says the unknown author of a little work, entitled *The Stars and the Earth*, in which these ideas were first developed, 'Thus the universe encloses the *pictures* of the past, like an indestructible and incorruptible record, containing the purest and the clearest truth ; and, as sound propagates itself in the air, wave after wave ; or, to take a still clearer example, as thunder and lightning are in reality simultaneous, but in the storm the distant thunder follows at the interval of seconds after the flash, so in like manner, according to our ideas, the pictures of every occurrence propagate themselves into the distant ether, upon the wings of a ray of light. And although they become weaker and smaller, yet, in immeasurable distance, they still have colour and form ; and, as everything possessing colour and form is visible, so must these pictures also be said to be visible, however impossible it may be for the human eye to perceive it with the hitherto discovered optical instruments.'—*Quotation in Hitchcock's 'Religion and Geology,'* Lect. xii.

What follows is Dr Hitchcock's own :—

'This photographic influence pervades all nature ; nor can we say where it stops. We do not know but it may imprint upon the world around us our features, as they are modified by various passions, and thus fill nature with daguerreotype impressions of all our actions that are performed in daylight.'

In the most ingenious way, he argues, from those processes of photography which demand *the exclusion of light*, that *the deeds of darkness* may be pictured as regularly as the deeds of light. And he calculates that the soul of the evil-doer may arrive at some planet destined to be his future dwelling-place, contemporaneously with the arrival, by the travelling light, of the pictured story of his life.

'The foulest enormities of human conduct have always striven to cover themselves with the shroud of night. The thief, the counterfeiter, the assassin, the robber, the murderer, and the seducer, feel comparatively safe in the midnight darkness, because no human eye can scrutinize their actions. But what if it should turn out that sable night, to speak paradoxically, is an unerring photographist! What if wicked men, as they open their eyes from the sleep of death in another world, should find the universe hung round with faithful pictures of their earthly enormities, which they had supposed for ever lost in the oblivion of night!'—*Religion and Geology*, Lect. xii.

But it seems to me, that there is no reality in such speculations. The chapter in Hitchcock's book on the *Telegraphic System of the Universe*, besides wearing the aspect of a hastily snatched induction, carries me away from the region where true awe and wonder dwell, into one where I can only admire the fancy of the writer. I would be sorry to have to believe, that this great universe which God made for His glory, should lower to a mere photographic record of human virtue or guilt. No! Our moral actions—as some one has truly said—vindicate or avenge themselves in our own being. The saintliness reveals the saint. The sin displays the sinner. At the judgment-day, the faith, which drew the souls of the righteous near to God in time, will demonstrate their nearness to Him for eternity. And equally, the unbelief, which put God far away, will exhibit unbelievers as far away themselves for ever. The awful 'Depart from Me' will be the mere natural response and embodiment of the sinner's own career.

> '*There* is no shuffling ; *there* the action lies
> In his true nature; and we ourselves compelled,
> Even to the teeth and forehead of our faults,
> To give in evidence.'

www.ingramcontent.com/pod-product-compliance
Lightning Source LLC
Chambersburg PA
CBHW031958230426
43672CB00010B/2197